THE

FIRST-TIME
MANAGER
DEI

THE
FIRST-TIME
MANAGER

DEI

DIVERSITY, EQUITY, & INCLUSION

ALIDA
MIRANDA-WOLFF

HarperCollins
Leadership

An Imprint of HarperCollins

Any internet addresses, phone numbers, or company or product information printed in this book are offered as a resource and are not intended in any way to be or to imply an endorsement by HarperCollins Leadership, nor does HarperCollins Leadership vouch for the existence, content, or services of these sites, phone numbers, companies, or products beyond the life of this book.

ISBN 978-1-4002-4610-6 (eBook)
ISBN 978-1-4002-4609-0 (TP)

Library of Congress Control Number: 2023948695

Printed in the United States of America
24 25 26 27 28 LBC 5 4 3 2 1

For my teammates—past, present, and future.

May all your hopes be realized.

CONTENTS

INTRODUCTION

THE FIRST TIME I EVER LED A MANAGEMENT CLASS, I played a music video called "Ladyboss." In the video, comedian and actress Rachel Bloom parodies #girlboss empowerment while also naming the very real struggles of managing others while navigating gender dynamics at work. I paused at the lyric "Take big swings and suppress the fear of catastrophic failure" to take the room's pulse. Much to my relief, my audience of first-time managers laughed in recognition. While we identified as different genders, races, ethnicities, life stages, and even specializations, we shared something vital in common: the ever-present pressure of being responsible for our employees' performance and experience at work.

Being a manager is often challenging, thankless, and confusing. This is a lesson I've learned several times over the course of my career. From the moment I graduated from college I knew I wanted to "be in charge." Unlike many of my peers, I did not come to management because of a lack of other career progression options or pressure from my organization or manager. I *wanted* to be a manager, partly because I had been led by some talented ones early on in my career. These were managers who, I would later learn, honed their craft because they came from marginalized groups and did not want to see the harm they had personally experienced reproduced. Naturally, as I navigated my career, I experienced my own biased managers and inequitable work environments; I also, unfortunately, acted on my biases and either unconsciously or misguidedly created exclusive work environments.

As a person who has been a manager longer than I have been anything else professionally, perhaps the most important lesson I've learned about management comes from an unexpected place. The theologian Paul Tillich, best known for his influence on his most famous pupil, Martin Luther King Jr., taught that power is the ability for a person to self-actualize, and love comes from wanting to be connected to something greater than oneself. Power without love can be abusive and selfish, while love without power can lead to the suppression of difference and the loss of self. It's my belief that being an inclusive manager means finding ways to balance power and love on a daily basis. When do we prioritize the needs of an individual employee over that of the whole team? When do we hold firm that what the team needs is more important than what the individual employee wants? How do we ensure that we respect one person's boundaries without compromising another's? How do we live up to the promises we make to ourselves and to each other, all while driving results and hitting our earnings targets?

These are not simple questions. In a world where social upheavals, individual experiences, and complex team dynamics come into constant contact, the answers we might have once held up as "right" leave much to be desired. Since management careers first came into being more than a century ago, managers have been faced with moving targets and rapid changes in what "good" management is. I don't pretend to have the definitive answer. Instead, I have an invitation: imagine what it would look like to cocreate a community of people who, by respecting and appreciating their differences, together achieve a sense of togetherness. What would it mean to nurture those conditions? To throw out the playbook of "standard, best practice" management, and instead, honor the humanity and dignity of those who you have been charged to bring together?

When offered the chance to contribute to *The First-Time Manager* series, I vowed to take everything I've learned about doing *that* kind of management and capture it in one place. These lessons come from the firsthand experiences of managing and being managed, secondhand learning through reading, research, and management training, and from my time as a coach and facilitator of diversity, equity, inclusion, and belonging management programs.

You don't need a PhD in googling to access information on inclusive management. What you want to know is out there. The real value in a project like *The First-Time Manager: Diversity, Equity & Inclusion* is not in the information itself but the work of guiding you in its application. That's my highest aspiration for this book—that it provides you with some insights, encouragement, and guidelines to help you do one of the hardest jobs there is, managing for the first time while cultivating a culture of belonging.

Alida Miranda-Wolff
May 31, 2023

PART ONE

THE ROLE OF AN INCLUSIVE MANAGER

INCLUSIVE MANAGEMENT IS ALL ABOUT embracing what makes someone a good manager—empathy, active listening, service orientation—and adapting these qualities to meet the needs of a diverse set of employees. Ultimately, as someone coming into your management role for the first time, *that* is your job.

1

GOOD MANAGERS

WHAT MAKES SOMEONE A GOOD MANAGER?

It's a question I ask at the start of every six-month inclusive management cohort I lead at my diversity, equity, inclusion, and belonging (DEIB) firm, Ethos. In response, participants volunteer a few consistent qualities. A good manager is "a good listener" and "goes out of their way to help." A good manager is "empathetic," "candid," and "personable." A good manager, above all else, "is transparent and trustworthy."

It's especially noteworthy what *isn't* reflected back; whether I am talking to a room full of software engineers or nonprofit fund-raisers, K–12 teachers, or waitstaff, hardly anyone focuses on how skilled, smart, or talented the manager is. I've never heard some-one say a good manager is a visionary thinker or a savant in a given field; rather, a good manager is mostly recognized for the welcoming, supportive environment they create and how they make their employees feel respected, valued, and understood.

This is not so when I ask what makes someone a bad manager, where "never listens," "stays away when things go wrong," and "keeps you in the dark" coexist with "incompetent," "oblivious," and "doesn't know how to do the work." We expect good managers to know how to do our jobs, our colleagues', and their own, and we expect them to be good at doing them. We value good managers for all of the ways they invest in making us feel seen, heard, and appreciated. The baseline for good managers is competence; it's all of the care, candor, and courage on top that elevates them. Which brings up another insight: good managers, the best managers, are not the protagonists or heroes in the story; they're the guides. They steer us away from failure and guide us down the path to success. Not everyone travels down the path to success the same way. Just as top-rated tour guides bring multiple stories, examples, and trip routes to work every day, so, too, does the new manager angling to make a lasting positive impact on their employees.

INCLUSIVE MANAGEMENT TIP ONE:
LEARN FROM SUCCESS

We often learn from success better than we do failure, though we are cognitively wired to remember failure more distinctly. As you consider how you will become an inclusive manager, observe other managers as they manage their teams. Keep an active log of their most effective, constructive behaviors and consider how you might implement them yourself.

You can access a sample log that includes examples of what to look for at **alidamirandawolff.com/bookreaders**.

2

EQUITABLE AND
INCLUSIVE MANAGERS

EMPLOYEES EXPECT TO HAVE A MANAGER who cares about and nurtures equity, makes sure there is diversity of identities on the team, and fosters a sense of inclusion and belonging among those team members.

You may already be familiar with terms like *diversity, equity, inclusion, cultural awareness, belonging, intersectionality,* and *microaggressions* but not how you are supposed to uphold them in your new manager role. Committing to memory some unified, clear definitions of what these things are, not to mention how they relate to your management practice, will help you meet expectations.

Diversity simply means variety, and it's specific to the composition of a group. At work, diversity means the presence of difference within our contained environments. Simply put, it's an outcome—you can clearly measure the variety of backgrounds, identities, and experiences on your team. When we have diversity on the teams we manage, we avoid gaps in our knowledge and perspectives that could lead to major issues.

Equity encompasses equal access and the meeting of individual needs. Equity is a set of processes that seeks to ensure that everyone on a team not only has the same opportunities as others, but that they can take advantage of them. For example, equity-minded managers understand that transparency through sharing key information with all team members is just the first step because equity comes from making sure everyone understands that information. If strong equity practices are in place, you can foster the experience of **inclusion**, which, like diversity, is an outcome.

Inclusion allows individuals with different identities to feel they are invited into the group because they are valued, relied upon, and welcomed. Inclusion is the beginning of a culture of belonging, since just because you feel invited into a group does not mean you take a place in it. That's why cultural awareness is so important.

Cultural awareness involves understanding the differences between us and people from other cultures or other backgrounds, especially differences in attitudes and values. Cultural awareness also involves becoming aware of our cultural values, beliefs, and perceptions to create space for those of others, usually by being willing to shift our own cultural context instead of asking others to assimilate. With diversity, equity, inclusion, and cultural awareness in place, we enable the conditions for belonging.

Belonging is the human emotional need to be an accepted member of a group. It is an experience many people have innately or inherently when with people just like them but is significantly harder to achieve in the presence of difference. The kind of belonging we focus on in this book is one that values, encourages, and nurtures diversity. In this context, belonging involves feeling part of something greater than yourself that values and respects you and that you value and respect back. Unfortunately, there are many barriers to experiencing belonging, including a failure to contemplate and respect intersectionality, implicit bias, hidden discrimination, and overt discrimination.

Specifically, **intersectionality** is a framework that allows us to understand how a person, group of people, or social problems are affected by a number of intersecting discriminations and disadvantages. When we view individual employees as only one category or identity, we erase whole elements of their experience, leaving them vulnerable to harm. That harm might come as a result of **implicit bias**, or the negative associations expressed automatically that people unknowingly hold and that affect understanding, actions, and decisions. When acted upon, implicit bias can show up as **hidden discrimination**, which is behavior that may not be intentionally discriminatory or is not perceived as such by the individuals doing the discriminating but may be perceived as offensive by the person being discriminated against. Or it can appear as more **overt discrimination**, defined as the unequal treatment of members of various groups based on conscious or unconscious prejudice, which favors one group over others based on differences of race, gender, economic class, sexual orientation, physical ability, religion, language, age, national identity, and other categories.

Your job is to take your awareness and knowledge of these ideas and experiences and flow them into your daily management and leadership practices, with a special emphasis on learning from those around you who hold different identities.

3

MANAGEMENT VERSUS LEADERSHIP

IN THE ORIGINAL *THE FIRST-TIME MANAGER*, the authors make a point to emphasize that not everyone will enjoy management. In fact, they suggest organizations host premanagement training for folks considering a management track with an "opt-out" at the end. Once you learn what goes into managing through an all-day or even all-week crash course, you let your company know if you want to do it with the expectation and full validation that "I don't" is an acceptable answer.

While a time- and labor-intensive crash course in management with no strings attached might seem like a waste, it's actually a brilliant antidote to a common problem: most of us have had managers who shouldn't have been managers at all. Whether because of lack of interest, lack of skill, or some combination of the two, these managers failed to reach the standards of their roles. Unfortunately, our current business culture conflates leadership and management, suggesting that they are the same, even when their central concerns and goals are not.

Managers hold teams, projects, and processes together, focusing on how to drive goals forward while also maintaining the systems and outcomes that came before them. A manager at an airline, for example, might make sure the plane takes off every day at the same time with a reliable crew and plenty of backup systems in case something goes wrong. When they do their jobs well, they are vital to the long-term functioning of teams, organizations, and cultures. When they don't, things fall apart.

Leaders, however, focus on making something by motivating others to make it with them. When whatever they envisioned is made, they move on to the next idea or product. They are focused on imagining the future, creating the new or novel, and taking lots of risks in the process. They inspire people to mobilize. They rely on capable managers to ensure that in the highly risky process of mobilizing people, those people feel safe, secure, and well tended.

Let's return to that airline analogy. If managers see to cultivating and supporting flight crews who make sure planes take off and stick to their routes and arrival times, leaders are the folks who dream up the planes before they are built, who take on exit door responsibilities when something goes wrong in flight, and lobby for the next iteration of air travel in the future. Without them, teams would rarely form or feel a clear sense of direction.

DIFFERENCES BETWEEN MANAGERS AND LEADERS	
MANAGERS	**LEADERS**
• Drive goals	• Drive vision
• Maintain what is here	• Build what is new
• Build systems and processes	• Build relationships
• Protect against risks	• Take risks
• Manage the day-to-day	• Manage the future
• Are measured on the work product of employees	• Are measured on the outcomes of the business

The reality is that most of us work in organizations that expect us to both lead and manage, even though our preferences and strengths may not align to these dual expectations. As the original *The First-Time Manager* authors put it, "The more you grow as a manager, the more you will be able to use leadership methods. As the workforce becomes better educated, informed, and transient, managers who are not also inspirational in their methods will be at a disadvantage."[1]

I genuinely like to both lead and manage, though I may gravitate toward one more than the other depending on what specific challenges arise in a given quarter. I have known many profoundly talented people who don't like to do either, their independence and sense of individual autonomy drawing them to other types of workplace relationships. And, of course, there are folks who develop skills in leadership over management or vice versa.

Assuming that you fall squarely in the category of being a person who is willing and committed to both lead and manage, having a basic framework will help you stay organized. Being a leader and manager requires navigating sometimes opposing perspectives and goals. If this is the path you aim to take, though, you have three overlapping responsibilities.

1. **Drive results:** Managers are measured based on how productive and successful their teams are. Leaders are measured based on how productive and successful their departments, business units, and overall organizations are. The effective leader-manager ensures their team members get the right things done on time, with the resources available to them and at the highest quality possible.

2. **Offer guidance:** To improve the existing processes and practices on the team, as well as develop team members, managers give and receive feedback, coach teammates and offer them guidance, and encourage their team members to do the same. Inclusive managers go out of their way to understand employees as protagonists in their own stories and ask how they can help their employees advance on their respective paths.

3. **Facilitate healthy teams:** To facilitate the development and flourishing of healthy teams, managers strategically

select, hire, onboard, and grow individual team members, ensure they are working together collaboratively, and offer multiple options for their growth and development. Inclusive managers also pay attention to team dynamics and foster healthy relationships.

4

THE SEVEN HABITS OF HIGHLY INCLUSIVE MANAGERS

AS MUCH AS THESE RESPONSIBILITIES ARE INTERCONNECTED, they also can come into conflict with one another. Facilitating a healthy team dynamic may compete with driving results if, in order to achieve that dynamic, you have to slow down and reset expectations. Similarly, offering guidance may involve helping a team member advocate for more control over an element of a project, which in turn leads to a breakdown in collaboration with a peer you didn't anticipate feeling threatened by this change. Attempting to balance these responsibilities is a daily practice, one that is especially hard when you have limited time and resources.

Luckily, there are seven behaviors (see figure 1) that help bridge the gap between these responsibilities and render them more compatible.

1. MODEL GROWTH-ORIENTED BEHAVIORS

2. HOLD YOURSELF AND OTHERS ACCOUNTABLE

3. SHARE INFORMATION AND CREATE CLARITY

4. PROACTIVELY ENGAGE IN HARD CONVERSATIONS

5. LEAD GROUP DYNAMICS

6. OFFER EMPLOYEES CARE

7. ADVANCE EQUITY AND BELONGING

FIGURE 1

1.
MODEL GROWTH-ORIENTED BEHAVIORS

Your employees look to you as their model for how to behave and succeed, regardless of how close your relationships to them may be. Simply by nature of spending time with you, they will start to take on some of your quirks, phrases, and characteristics. In a previous role, I made a point to celebrate my employees' birthdays on a big day with elaborate celebration cakes, balloon banners, and neatly arranged wrapped gifts. Then, I noticed something interesting. An employee who previously said they were "terrible about remembering birthdays" scheduled, planned, and hosted a team celebration for her intern. She was watching me for cues, taking what she thought was worthwhile, and then replicating my behaviors.

To drive results while still nurturing a culture of feedback and collaboration, you must demonstrate your own growth-oriented and balanced behaviors on your team. As much as "show, don't tell" is a cliché, it's important to remember that how you show up determines how your employees will too. If you want your employees to work together as a team, you have to show them what that looks like by modeling it yourself.

- How are you collaborating with your peers?
- How would someone outside of your peer group know that the collaboration was taking place?
- What do you say about your peers to your employees?

These questions might help keep you accountable to practicing what you ask of others.

2.
HOLD YOURSELF
AND OTHERS ACCOUNTABLE

Many new managers find that they have difficulty holding others accountable. For one, most likely you advanced into a management role because you had a knack for holding yourself accountable—self-managed people are often rewarded with more responsibility. If you work with others who don't have that same sense of internal accountability, guiding them can be especially difficult because it's hard to teach something you know inherently.

To hold others accountable, start by pinpointing how they respond to expectations. Do they meet expectations they set for themselves, or ones set by others? Perhaps they meet both types of expectations. Or they may have a more rebellious spirit and reject expectations altogether, opting for values-based or desire-driven forms of accountability. Nevertheless, part of your role as a manager is to identify, without judgment, what your employees' responses to expectations are and tailor accountability structures accordingly.

An employee who is more internally motivated by expectations may need context in order to feel accountable. If you notice they ask several questions before committing to a task or try to collect information ahead of a major decision, help them set up accountability strategies that bake in time to learn about a given area and tie back to their own individual or personal goals. For an employee who is responsive to others' expectations more than their own, focus on who will be affected by their work and consider pairing them with a peer to meet major milestones.[1]

Importantly, do not ask your employees to be accountable to you if you are not accountable to them. Mutuality is key. I spoke with an operations manager who was having trouble making it to meetings on time. My first guess was that this individual was burned out and needed a sabbatical; however, upon closer inspection, I found that the employee was mirroring the department head's behavior. He had a tendency to join meetings twenty to thirty minutes late, cancel them a few minutes after they were set to start, or just not show up at all. His behavior set the standard for the team, including for this operations manager. The problem was that to contribute to the broader organization, this behavior needed to be unlearned.

3.
SHARE INFORMATION
AND CREATE CLARITY

The more a worker moves up in an organization, the more access to information they have. Managers often underestimate the sizable difference between how much more they know about their organizations than their employees do. As a manager, take time to understand what your employees do and do not know about how the team works, the business operates, and the industry is evolving and changing over time.

A mentee shared with me that one of the hardest parts about being a first-generation college student and first-generation white-collar worker was that they were missing so much background information. They grew up on a Native reservation where their parents mainly worked in the world of cattle. With few mentors and even fewer people to ask basic questions about workplace protocol, they felt unsure of themselves in an office setting. Should they just know what a P&L (profit and loss statement) was? Should they want to see their organization's, or would that be inappropriate at this level? And, working at a venture-funded firm that wasn't profitable, how could they connect the dots between their role of generating revenue as an account representative and the fact that the majority of the organization's revenue came from something other than sales?

Every employee you manage should know how the organization makes money, how much the company needs to make, and how their role is related to both. If you don't have these answers, get them, and find a way to lay them out in easy-to-understand terms that any new or tenured employee could digest. Don't take for granted they know this information by default.

4.
PROACTIVELY ENGAGE IN HARD CONVERSATIONS

In my book *Cultures of Belonging: Building Inclusive Organizations That Last*, I wrote that good leaders have an open-door policy, but great leaders walk the halls. This is especially true of hard conversations, whether you are initiating a mediation between two of your employees who have fallen out, sharing condolences with a team member who recently lost a child, or acknowledging a major moment of social upheaval. Much of your role as a manager revolves around anticipating and responding—being proactive—rather than reacting in the moment.

My general guideline is that, as much as possible, be the one to initiate the conversation rather than the last to be brought into it. This is especially important when it comes to conflict, grief, or distress. Proactively share leave policies, offer support in challenging client meetings, and bring sidebar conversations into your all-team meeting. Make it known that "pass" is always an option so folks who don't want to take that leave or aren't ready to bring you into the meeting have a sense of agency. Don't make assumptions.

5.
LEAD GROUP DYNAMICS

Never forget that one of your primary roles as manager is to ensure the team operates smoothly. That means that until you have a firm grounding established, you own meeting formats, assign out work, and set the standards for review. How the team works together is just as important as whether they do, and that is squarely in your job description.

Leading group dynamics, though, requires a certain amount of communal decision-making and accommodation. Don't just write a guide to accessible meetings without first talking to your employees about how they define accessibility, what tools they use that most benefit them, what tools the team currently uses that don't provide value, and what their expectations are of their own participation in the meetings. You *guide* the team; you don't control it. You are here to make their collective functioning smoother and more streamlined, not to run a mini fiefdom with you in the noble person's seat.

6.
OFFER EMPLOYEES CARE

To offer care is to help people meet their needs. This makes care context dependent. If you manage a team of nurses, the way you offer them care will be different from how they offer their patients care. A nurse reporting to you doesn't need you to take their temperature or check their oxygen level, but they may need you to rework the staffing schedule after they've worked two back-to-back shifts.

Employee needs and organizational results frequently clash. If the business goal is to reduce costs and the employee need is for the average hourly salary to increase by three dollars, managers may find themselves in the unhappy position of choosing sides. As an inclusive manager, you owe it to yourself and your teammates to make the case that the three-dollar increase will improve results, and then find other ways to reduce costs.

Propose that pay increase alongside a dramatic cut in consultancy and vendor fees, talk to employees about what they most need beyond pay increases if the company won't budge, and use the power you do have to create a more helpful, considerate environment.

7.
ADVANCE EQUITY AND BELONGING

Equity in management involves ensuring the same baseline resources are equally accessible to all and that each individual can take advantage of those resources. Providing training on reading a profit and loss statement, for example, is the first stage of an equitable management process. Making sure that a custom FAQ, office hours, and one-on-one conversations take place to account for the fact that for some this will be more familiar than others is the complete cycle.

Equity is how we take a group of diverse people and make them feel included, appreciated, and like they belong. When individuals experience belonging at work, they feel part of something greater than themselves that values and respects them and that they value and respect back. Belonging requires the **"three Rs"** of relationships, resources, and reciprocity.

Relationships are the cornerstone of belonging. Specifically, belonging cannot happen in a vacuum; it's a fundamentally relational experience. We must feel connected to one or more people to belong, so if we work on teams in which we don't know one another or can't invest time in deepening our relationships to one another, belonging will most likely evade us.

That's why resources are so important. We need at least the bare minimum of time, energy, and mental space to develop bonds with our colleagues. We may also need physical space, technology, or tools to create a sense of connection across locations and time zones. Of course, if we know we are underpaid relative to our peers or don't make a living wage, then we also most likely won't experience belonging because we don't feel valued or respected.

Finally, reciprocity is what makes us feel part of something greater, and the idea of give-and-take—mutual respect and value— is baked into the definition. Reciprocity is the practice of exchange. If I am an employee who gives all of my free time and energy to my team and my team doesn't support me when I need them, I will feel isolated and alone. We feel a more profound sense of belonging when we know we can rely on one another, when we can all feel needed and express needs.

5

THE STAGES OF MANAGEMENT

NOW THAT WE HAVE ESTABLISHED WHAT makes a good and inclusive manager, it's time to break down the more granular roles and responsibilities involved in management.

Managers oversee the employee life cycle. From hiring and interviewing, onboarding and training, and day-to-day supervision to navigating change, improving performance, and handling voluntary and involuntary departures, managers focus on the employee experience and their team's overall performance. Management is a full-service role; you are responsible for all things related to your team and its members' entrances and exits.

INTERVIEWING AND HIRING

Interviewing and hiring is one of your largest management responsibilities. Depending on your organization, you may own some or all of the parts of a recruitment process, from writing the first job description and selecting the hiring team to conducting interviews and extending an offer. Make sure that no matter what components of this process you manage, you actively focus on eliminating bias from application screenings and interview questions and use a scorecard to rate candidates rather than just going on your "gut." You can find more resources on equitable and inclusive hiring practices at alidamirandawolff.com/bookreaders.

ONBOARDING AND TRAINING

After you extend an offer and receive a signed offer letter in return, you are responsible for onboarding a new employee and training them about the company, the team, and in their function. Any complete onboarding plan should come directly from you with input from the new employee's peers holding comparable positions. It should also span at least ninety days (though the average employee won't be done onboarding until they have been with an organization for six months).

Training does not stop with onboarding, and employees undergoing any sort of transition, enrichment, and increased responsibilities should routinely go through new training. They should also revisit trainings from six or more months before to prevent the inevitable amnesia that comes with doing a lot of work daily while not keeping training concepts and lessons in active rotation. Managers make and deliver training, partner with other teams and team leaders for subjects outside their knowledge sphere or skill set, and bring in still more trainers to help address multiple learning and processing styles.

DAY-TO-DAY SUPERVISION

When I first started managing, I never imagined that the most time-intensive component of the work would be assigning tasks, reviewing work products, troubleshooting issues, and approving everything from external-facing emails to two-hundred-page reports. Day-to-day supervision is the bulk of management, not just in terms of an employee's tenure if they stay past the onboarding phase but also in terms of sheer work hours. Make sure that in all of your daily interactions and supervision of your employees, you are using the results, guidance, and team dynamics framework to ensure you are meeting your own goals.

NAVIGATING CHANGE

There are people who manage customers, products, marketing messages, and more. Sometimes those people are also managing other humans. What I know for sure, though, is that all managers engage in some form of change management, where they prepare others for change, build the vision and plan for it, implement it, embed it into the culture, and measure its results at the end. For every major transition that affects your team, you will manage its impacts, whether you do so intentionally or not.

For example, if your organization introduces a new customer relationship management system, getting your employees to use it is a management process on its own. Their level of adoption, compliance, usage, and efficiency will have as much to do with how well they were trained as with the work you put into getting them to use the platform as intended. There's a reason "change management" is a field of study and, in some organizations, a designated occupation.

PERFORMANCE AND IMPROVEMENT

Most employees have two questions for their managers, whether they ask them explicitly or not. "How am I doing?" (their individual performance) and "How are we doing?" (the health of your working relationship). Employees want to know if they are good at their jobs, meeting expectations, and delivering on their promises. They also want to know if you like working with them, are on good terms with them, and are committed to investing in a relationship with them.

Your job as an inclusive new manager is to anticipate these questions, set explicit measurements for them, address your own biases and privileges, and recognize your employees' identities and related needs as you do. It's also necessary to provide them the answers to these questions early and often so they can contribute meaningfully to the team.

TERMINATION

Termination can be the hardest stage of management. When an employee resigns or retires, which is called **voluntary termination**, a manager is responsible for their full transition process. This involves communicating the news and fielding questions, transitioning their work and delegating their responsibilities, processing separation paperwork, and other key logistic components.

Involuntary termination, which includes layoffs and firings, may be more complicated depending on the circumstances, such as the employee response, what the circumstances that led to the decision were, and whether the termination can or could be prevented with the right interventions. In either form of termination, you will likely partner with human resources or your leadership team to understand your role and the tasks you must complete.

6

UNDERSTANDING YOUR POWER

NO MATTER WHO YOU ARE OR HOW YOU IDENTIFY, if you are a manager, you hold power. After all, **power** is simply being able to do what you want to do or have others do what you want them to do. Your power is not total—you likely have to do things you don't want or have control over, and your employees may not always heed your advice or follow your directions. Nevertheless, the reality is that you are in charge of other people, which means, whether you like it or not, you hold power over them.

Having this power is not something to be ashamed of or afraid of, nor is it something to take lightly. Being an inclusive manager means accepting that power is inherently neutral; what makes it good or bad is how it's used. You must accept and name your power to use it responsibly.

Depending on the management setup in your organization, you will likely have the power to:

- influence the addition and selection of new team members;
- set goals;
- define the roles and responsibilities of employees;
- assign work and projects;
- review employee performance;

- approve paid time off, such as vacation time and sick time, as well as leave time;
- recommend and make promotions; and
- make terminations.

Knowing that you have power over those you manage, you are in the unique position of being able to think deeply about when to use it, how to share it, and when to give it up to someone else. Some guiding questions can help you consider what to do when designing and leading an equitable, inclusive team.

- Is there room to make this decision together? Am I making a decision *for* someone when I could make it *with* them?
- Am I the best person to make this decision? Why or why not?
- Does everyone on my team understand why I used my power in this particular way? What would I need to show, share, or do for this to happen?
- Do I use my power to advance team goals and interests?
- Do I use my power to give credit, acknowledge, and support the development of those I have power over?

Employees aren't powerless. Within some diversity, equity, inclusion, and belonging circles, the concept of "empowering others" reads as patronizing and elitist. Employees come into an organization with power. Managers don't need to transform their employees from powerless people into empowered ones. Every one of your employees has their own voice; the issue is whether others listen when they use that voice. Your role is to do what you can to make sure others listen when your employees advocate for themselves.

You are a megaphone, not a mouthpiece—you amplify others' voices rather than replacing theirs with your own.

Your employees also have power over you. You need them even though you have power over them. Some employees will understand this more intuitively than others. This can manifest in a variety of ways. For example, just because you delegate a task doesn't mean your employee will complete it. Employees who dislike your management style may report dissatisfaction to *your* manager, human resources, or organizational leaders. If your employee disagrees with a policy you put in place, they may violate it, either unintentionally or intentionally. More generally, employees have the power to withhold their labor altogether. They can work less or stop working completely.

At the system level, **employee power** is a net positive. Think of their ability to say no or refuse to work as a kind of check and balance in a work environment. If leaders break their promises and exploit their workers, those workers can strike, quit, sue, or take any number of other group actions. You might count yourself among these workers if you find your rights have been violated or if you choose to stand in solidarity with your colleagues. Nevertheless, at the interpersonal level, how your employees exercise their power can be damaging or destructive. In more than one situation, I have found myself working until one or two in the morning because an employee missed a deadline and told me at the last minute; some of those employees were apologetic and vowed to do better next time, while others told me to get over it and accept that their needs were more important than mine. The way individual employees exercise their power is especially challenging when it directly affects their peers. If they fail to meet expectations or take on their tasks, it often has consequences on another person's workload, anxiety level, and self-estimation. Using your power as a manager responsibly also means observing how your team members use theirs and reminding, guiding, and directing them in making decisions that consider collective well-being.

7

SETTING HEALTHY BOUNDARIES

SETTING BOUNDARIES IS PERHAPS THE MOST VALUABLE and least talked about management skill in the inclusive manager's tool kit. **Boundaries**, which are short for emotional boundaries, are the property lines that separate your thoughts and feelings from those of other people. Managing teams successfully is tied up with managing boundaries—yours, theirs, everybody's—adeptly and sensitively.

VIOLATING BOUNDARIES

When someone violates our boundaries, they enter our unprotected or unguarded space without our permission. This may mean asking overly personal questions, confiding a secret we did not ask to know, or even inappropriately touching us. The point is that the closeness or intimacy is not two-way, and we did not elect to take part in it.

Imagine that you and three of your direct reports are at a bowling alley for a team-building activity where you all hope to improve your bowling game. Each person has their own lane. As the team's manager, it's your job to make sure that folks aren't tossing their bowling balls haphazardly across lanes, knocking over other people's sets of pins. In a best-case scenario, the person whose lane has been invaded doesn't mind but also doesn't learn how to consistently get strikes or improve their game. Having their boundaries crossed can deprive them of developing necessary skills or operating without the peer bowling for them.

In a worst-case scenario, the person throwing their ball across lanes miscalculates and accidentally knocks over their colleague rather than the bowling pins. The boundary violation results in harm, which might in turn cause unhealthy, unproductive conflict. Even if they don't toss their bowling ball at their colleague, they might still provoke frustration, discomfort, or harm. In any of these cases, ignoring boundaries or not setting them at all has negative repercussions. These repercussions might be more severe if, instead of this exchange happening between colleagues, it takes place between you and your employee. As someone with more power over an employee's future than the average peer, your ability to do harm is significantly greater.

OVERSETTING BOUNDARIES

Much of the conversation around setting boundaries focuses on what to do when there aren't enough of them. Having too many or holding them too tightly, though, poses a unique set of problems. If you are responsible for creating a warm, welcoming, and supportive team environment, a culture of overly rigid boundaries may get in the way.

So, we're back at the bowling alley. The whole reason you planned this event was that members of the team said they wanted to bond over a shared activity, agreed bowling was a fun, easy way to do that, and confided they wanted to improve as bowlers. Then you get to the bowling alley and one of your team members chooses a lane five lanes over from everyone else's. The whole time, they bowl by themselves and avoid conversation and eye contact with their teammates, even though they agreed this would be an ideal team-bonding activity. You ask them if something is wrong, and they say they simply prefer to bowl alone. When you suggest they might share some of their bowling knowledge and prowess with their teammates, they firmly decline. "My bowling knowledge is mine, and no one else is entitled to it. I won't share it." But when they notice another teammate consistently getting strikes, they ask for that employee's secret to the perfect spin. After receiving an answer, they return to their faraway lane, perfecting their game without sharing their learnings with anyone else.

What's happening here? An overly rigid boundary has eliminated the possibility of mutuality and the experience of give-and-take. Team members go from thinking of collective wins and gains to only individual ones. What's worse, some team members continue to give their time, energy, and knowledge to others without receiving help or support in return. Not only is this unfair on an interpersonal level, it creates the conditions for exclusion.

Who gets to set such strong boundaries is often socially conditioned. For one, if you as the manager are setting this boundary, you are reinforcing the idea that you have power and privilege over others that you can use for your own gain and to their detriment. If this experience of you becomes the default, your team will not be a welcoming and supportive place, especially because others are looking to you as the example for what "good behavior" on the team looks like.

Social identity factors here too. For those socialized as girls or women, setting boundaries is often conflated with being selfish, grasping, and uncaring, while those socialized as boys or men may not have any negative associations with setting firm boundaries. Similarly, employees raised in more collectivist cultures versus those raised in more independent ones might find themselves working a lot more and doing the hardest, most thankless tasks under the mistaken assumption that others will show up for them in their time of need. This is a recipe for resentment, cynicism, and burnout. Finally, employees subjected to the **model minority myth**, which often affects Asian Americans, can feel pressured to take on more work, suppress their needs, or counterbalance their "problematic" peers who raise flags about unjust or inequitable treatment. This burden may or may not offer more professional opportunities in the short term but almost always at a cost.

ESTABLISHING EFFECTIVE BOUNDARIES

Whether a boundary is too firm or not firm enough, the same core issue is at stake: trust. If, as Rachel Botsman writes in *Who Can You Trust? How Technology Brought Us Together and How It Might Drive Us Apart*, trust is a "confident relationship with the unknown," then unclear and unequal boundaries threaten everyone's ability to navigate ambiguity, a vital skill in fast-paced, rapidly changing environments like workplaces.

To set your team on the right course, model these basic boundary-setting behaviors yourself.

Probe the Reasons for Feeling Overwhelmed. When you feel overwhelmed or unfocused, ask yourself if you feel this way because you are not honoring or holding an appropriate boundary or because someone else is failing to do so. Ask your employees the same question and help them probe if you see them struggling to arrive at an answer. If you find that either you or your employees are experiencing boundary-related stress and resentment, consider:

- What is the boundary not being honored?
- Why isn't the boundary being honored? Does it have to do with unspoken rules, a need for approval or validation, mismatched expectations, or something else?
- What would an appropriate boundary look like?

- How might that boundary be set, asserted, loosened, or eliminated, depending on what it is?

Be Clear About Needs. Share your feelings and experiences with your team around your workplace needs. For example, if employees are consistently turning in work for your review only hours before a deadline and it's stressing you out, tell them. How much you share is up to you, but you should not keep this to yourself. Some things you might offer are that you need processing time to take in new information, so such a tight turnaround creates a significant cognitive load. Or, that you manage your working hours very carefully to create space in your day for your many caregiving responsibilities.

Make sure you are sharing for the purposes of deeper learning, not to feel taken care of or fulfilled by others. If you feel inclined toward complaining or commiserating, or you notice a hidden desire to make others feel guilty, pause. How would any of those responses lead to the future strength of the team? How would they affect the way others set, hold, and honor boundaries? When your team members struggle with boundaries and their teammates, use yourself as an example for the naming and negotiation of needs openly and without hesitation.

It's also important to pay attention to *whom* you ask to meet your needs. Do you find yourself defaulting to the same person or people on your team over and over again? Why? And do they hold particular social identities associated with offering care, such as marginalized genders, caregivers, or others with nondominant identities?

Practice Saying No. No is the easiest boundary. When you are struggling with a team that doesn't set enough boundaries, emphasize that no is an option, and it's one that may not even require explanation. An appropriate and, yes, kind response to a question like, "I'm going out for drinks with a few friends and colleagues. Are you coming?" is "No." It's a complete sentence. Though, of course, if you are worried about oversetting a boundary, you are welcome to explain why you are declining.

Refer Outside Help. If an employee struggles with difficult emotions, managers can default to oversetting their own boundaries out of a fear that they will fall into the uncomfortable and unmanageable role of "work therapist." Your employees will experience grief, frustration, loneliness, and anger at work, whether it's because of things happening outside of the office or inside of it. You have a responsibility to respond with attention and care. Depending on the situation, you do not have a responsibility to "fix" or counsel them through the situation.

Let's say an employee discloses they are going through a painful divorce. Instead of offering relationship guidance or spending hours talking about the heartbreak of separation, consider where you have power and how you could use it to help. Remind the employee, "We offer an Employee Assistance Program with access to information, services, and support that could help." Suggest, "If you need outside support, we can adjust your schedule to be more flexible." And, if you have the connections available, you may even consider extending introductions to peer communities of folks navigating life transitions and career growth at the same time.

Set an Equitable Practice. If the difficult emotions employees express are directly related to identity-based systems of inequality, don't overset a boundary by suggesting that making a change is beyond your role. It isn't. Equity practices are about simultaneously improving access to resources and making sure everyone can take advantage of them, especially those who may have been conditioned not to know how.

An employee struggling with addiction or violence at home may not qualify for leave under your existing policies; advocate for a new policy among your human resources and leadership teams while also using your discretionary powers over paid time off and sick time to support that employee. If one of your team members explains that they routinely feel left out or disregarded because of their neurodivergence, work with them to identify different communication practices and techniques they would like the team to adopt, such as asynchronous meetings or the incorporation of captioning software. Once it's established as a regular practice, hard code it into your team's way of doing things so that it's an organic part of workflows.

To earn one another's trust, every person on your team has to first be transparent, making as much known about their work styles, expectations, and commitments as possible early on, and then proving those things to be true over time so that when clear answers aren't available, everyone feels safe.

8

HOW NOT TO MANAGE

MY COLLEAGUE KARYN OATES, a highly skilled manager in her own right, has said that preserving her humanity as a worker has always been intertwined with knowing and setting her boundaries. There is so much wisdom in this statement, especially for new managers. In teaching my course on management for change agents, I ask for participants to bring specific examples of management challenges they are currently facing. About two-thirds usually relate to boundaries, either setting too strong a boundary (rigidity) or not enough of one (overaccommodation). Five of the most common management pitfalls also happen to be tied to boundaries.

You may need to revisit your relational boundaries if you:

1. **Hold on to the work you did before you were a manager.** Here's the thing about managing other people: your responsibility shifts from just having to worry about getting yourself in order to helping many other people do just that. It's time consuming and energetically expensive. As tempting as it can be to hold on to all of the tasks you did as an individual contributor, the reality is that, very quickly, you will go from being in charge of your own to-do list to having to manage unplanned work from everyone

else's to-do lists. Your number one job is to advise the team, which likely means delegating work to others.

2. **Function as a confidant, life coach, or parent to your employees.** Americans spend one-third of their lives working, which means that for some of your employees, their deepest and most consistent relationships are organizational ones. With loneliness on the rise, especially among millennial and Gen Z workers, the problem of seeking social, emotional, and psychological fulfillment *exclusively* from work is not going away. As a manager, you must clearly define what your role is and what it is not, both for your own well-being and theirs. You hold power over your employees—you decide if they are promoted or fired, what projects they work on, when they can take time off, and so much more. It's not good for either of you to forget who you are to each other, even if you still cultivate a warm, trusting, and fulfilling relationship.

3. **Maintain the same level of close relationships with your direct reports as they did when you were peers.** After reading that last behavior, you may be wondering: "But what do I do if we used to be peers and this power dynamic is new?" First, let's debunk a common work myth. You can be friends with people you work with; in fact, chances are you will stay at your organization longer if you do have friends among your colleagues. But you must name the new power dynamic with those employees you have preexisting relationships with and outline what can stay the same and what cannot. For example, maybe when you were peers, you would commiserate about that one insensitive colleague. Now, that colleague isn't at your same level; they report to you. As a manager, you can listen, but you can't commiserate with your employee about another person who works for you without introducing bias, favoritism, and harmful communication structures as part of the team culture.

4. **Measure success only by your own outputs, as opposed to those of your teammates.** Good managers exist to drive results across teams. If you succeed at your individual tasks and your team underperforms, you underperform. Remember that team wins *are* your wins.

5. **Choose artificial harmony over healthy conflict.** Conflict can be uncomfortable, disruptive, and counterproductive. Yet, when engaged properly, it often helps advance shared goals, uncover root issues, and identify areas and methods of repair. The temptation to leave what's potentially provocative or conflict laden unspoken or unaddressed is natural. But just because it's natural doesn't mean it's useful. Resist the impulse to avoid conflict, and choose resolution over denial.

9

DEVELOPING YOUR
MANAGEMENT STYLE

UNDERSTANDING YOUR POWER, SETTING HEALTHY BOUNDARIES, and identifying behaviors and practices to avoid are all parts of one of the most important projects you will undertake in your career: developing your management style. Your reactions to each of these ideas and how you decide to implement them will actually tell you more about what that style is than any quiz or assessment you might take. Quizzes and assessments are valuable because, although we might intrinsically know what our style is, describing and improving that style is another thing entirely. Categories help us identify our natural preferences while pinpointing how we might reach the pinnacle of our management skills.

Daniel Goleman, author of *Emotional Intelligence*, and Korn Ferry developed a Leadership Styles Survey to identify six leadership styles managers can use on teams to drive performance. As you read through the descriptions, ask yourself a few questions:

- Which of these styles most resonates with me and how do I prefer to manage?

- Where might I need to try a different approach in order to create a more inclusive environment for different team members?
- What would it look like to blend multiple styles into a regular, working management practice?

VISIONARY

Visionary leaders define the ideal future, but they do not prescribe how to get there. Setting a long-term purpose for the team creates clarity. Eschewing short-term mandates around achieving that purpose allows team members the creativity and freedom to experiment. Team members who have trouble envisioning the future or have not yet learned how to develop their own action plans or participate in brainstorming may feel uncomfortable under a visionary leader. With employees who have historically been shut down, silenced, or told their ideas (whether implicitly or explicitly) aren't important, you will need to earn their trust before they fully engage with this style. Generally, team members with visionary leaders report having shared goals and a strong positive sentiment toward their organizational missions.

COACHING

Coaching leaders take a personalized approach to upskilling their team members, resulting in long-term strategic capabilities. These leaders play the long game, trusting that investing in their team members will pay off down the road. Coaching leaders preoccupy themselves with understanding everyone's strengths, areas for improvement, and aspirations. They use this knowledge to unlock potential. The coaching style is a sophisticated leadership style and therefore underused. You must have team members in touch with their goals and dreams or this style might feel frustrating for them as they struggle to name their aims. A coaching style is especially important for more mature or experienced teams with subject-matter expertise so that they remain engaged and committed to new possibilities within a familiar role or organization.

AFFILIATIVE

Affiliative leaders go out of their way to express care and interest in their teammates, and they dedicate time and energy to creating a harmonious, warm, and welcoming environment. This style relies highly on encouragement and recognition. Leaders who use an affiliative leadership style make their employees feel valued not only as workers but as people. Affiliative leaders fail when they confuse care with conflict avoidance, choosing not to address underperformance or missed expectations out of a desire to promote harmony. Artificial harmony only sows distrust and doubt among team members. Affiliative leadership in combination with a commitment to honesty is stabilizing, supportive, and capable of creating the conditions for long-lasting relationships.

PARTICIPATIVE

Participative leaders focus on generating consensus among employees through shared goal setting, visioning, and decision-making. Participative leaders encourage group responsibility and accountability. Involving team members in the project of shaping their environments creates a great deal of personal ownership, team pride, and long-term buy-in. But it's time consuming and may be challenging to navigate during times of crisis or conflict. Participative leadership also requires significant trust, not only between you and your team members but among the team members themselves. As a result, participative leadership is most successful on teams with low turnover and strong feedback cultures. Teams where there aren't many people coming or going and radical candor is the norm thrive with participative leaders.

PACESETTING

Pacesetting leaders set and meet their own high standards, exemplifying the quality, pace, and output they hope to see from their employees. These leaders have the ability to get into the work in moments of need, and they are not afraid to show rather than tell. The downside of pacesetting is that, without proper guidance, this style can make employees feel inadequate and leave them unprepared to solve problems on their own. Pacesetting leaders also set ambitious, challenging goals that may not feel attainable, leading to lower employee sentiment. Used in certain contexts—to solve an unexpected problem, meet a fast-approaching deadline, or respond to a shift in climate—it galvanizes and emboldens team members while also creating a sense among employees that their manager is an active participant in the team's day-to-day work.

DIRECTIVE

Like the pacesetting leadership style, directive leadership is valuable in moderation. **Directive leaders** tell employees what to do and how to do it, which results in alignment and clarity. Unmonitored directive leadership—a form many of us have experienced with our own bosses—is demanding, controlling, and criticism heavy. It also has the misfortune of being associated with a "Because I said so" approach to communication, which grates more often than it inspires. Directive leaders are effective when there is limited time, many moving parts and unknown variables, and high levels of uncertainty on the team. They can provide structure to teams failing due to structurelessness, and if combined with positive encouragement and active listening, can be well received by employees.

Now that you know all six of the leadership styles, consider trying out different leadership styles on the team and noting how employees respond. While keeping your own boundaries in mind, tailor some of your everyday practices to their needs.

INCLUSIVE MANAGEMENT TIP TWO: CRAFT A MANAGEMENT STATEMENT

Imagine your highest vision of yourself as a manager. Write down a few sentences about what being a caring, inclusive, and just manager means to you, including what practices you might employ on a daily, weekly, monthly, and annual basis. Take some time to edit whatever you came up with into an easy-to-remember statement, preferably no more than six sentences. Then, print it out and frame it, use it as a desktop background, make it your phone home screen, or do all three! Whenever you are faced with management decisions, challenges, or even questions, go back to this statement and use it to help guide your next actions.

PART TWO

CREATING A CULTURE OF BELONGING

AS A MANAGER, you have an explicit mandate to make sure your team is cohesive, collaborative, and connected. Specifically, you ought to spend real time and effort making sure people feel they *belong* on your team, which will ultimately lead to fewer departures, better quality work, and stronger positive sentiments, not to mention healthier workplace relationships.

10

THE PROBLEM OF WORKPLACE LONELINESS

SINCE AT LEAST THE 1980S, researchers and management experts alike have been studying the impact of loneliness on quality of life, outlook, and performance. Judging by multiple US surgeons general calling loneliness an "epidemic," you've likely at least heard of the problems loneliness poses for individuals, communities, and whole cultures.

In 2020, Cigna's Loneliness Index revealed that three out of five Americans consider themselves lonely, a 7 percent increase from 2018. Not only that, but work and loneliness are directly connected, with lonely workers reporting higher rates of absenteeism, lower rates of engagement and productivity, and a higher likelihood of both considering quitting and going through with it. Moreover, remote workers are more likely to be lonely than ones working in an office, an especially challenging problem considering that remote work has been shown to especially benefit caregivers, disabled people, and people of color in other ways.

It's worth noting that *being lonely* and *being alone* are not the same thing. Being alone is a neutral state, one that some of your employees may prefer. Being lonely, however, is a negative state. When you feel lonely, there is a gap between your expectations ("I want to feel connected to others") and your experience ("I don't feel connected to anyone"). Your goal as a manager is not to make sure people who keep to themselves or work independently are always in collaboration mode. Instead, it's to create the conditions for people to feel an alignment between their social expectations and experiences.

11

WHAT IS BELONGING?

TO CREATE THESE CONDITIONS, you first need to understand what belonging is. While I write extensively about belonging and how to make sure you're creating the structures on your team to make it possible in my first book, *Cultures of Belonging: Building Inclusive Organizations That Last*, we'll stick to the basics here.

Belonging researchers in the 1990s defined the psychologically necessary experience of belongingness as "To belong is to matter; sense of belonging enhances meaning in life."[1] Belonging can happen only in a relationship—you cannot belong on your own. Rather, you need to feel that you matter to others and are part of a group or community. Through this experience, you can feel more connected to your own sense of purpose or reason for being in the world.

As described in part 1, **belonging** is feeling as though you are part of something greater than yourself that values and respects you and that you value and respect back. What belonging isn't, despite its misleading name, is ownership. While objects might belong to us, people do not. Belonging becomes grasping, toxic, and unjust when members feel compelled to act against their beliefs or values in order to fit in or meet the demands of their group. That's why it is so important that we talk about creating the conditions for belonging rather than making someone belong.

Ultimately, whether someone belongs should be up to them, a matter of their choice. What inclusive managers are responsible for is making a compelling case to make that choice, but in no way should they lay claim to the people they manage. The healthy, constructive kind of belonging comes from the practice of three competencies, which I call the "Three Rs."

THE THREE Rs

The Three Rs are relationships, resources, and reciprocity. By developing practices around all three belonging competencies, you can continuously develop and strengthen the experience of belonging on your team.

Relationships are the cornerstone of belonging. Remember, people can't experience belonging by themselves. Belonging happens on teams when employees feel they can have meaningful relationships with one another. An employee who believes they have meaningful relationships with their colleagues will say things like:

- "My teammates see me as a whole person, not just an employee."
- "I can show up as myself and my teammates will accept and appreciate who I am."
- "I have things in common with my teammates, including shared goals and values."
- "I am able to make decisions for myself without fear that my teammates will retaliate against me."
- "I feel safe when I am among my teammates, even when I hold different opinions or we are in conflict."
- "When I articulate my needs to my teammates, those needs are validated and respected."

- "If something goes wrong, I know I can rely on my teammates to help me."

Resources refer to all the things employees need to be able to make these statements. For example, if I am scheduled for back-to-back meetings every day and under pressure to stick to a structured agenda, it will be harder for me to get to know my teammates or be known by them. Similarly, even if I do have the time to check in or engage in social conversations with my colleagues, if I am under an overwhelming amount of stress or experiencing too many competing priorities, it's unlikely that I will be fully present with them. The phenomenon of being distracted or multitasking while trying to connect is well known by device users of all kinds. Can you really develop trust with someone if every time you're listening to them, you are also checking emails on your phone and notifications on your computer?

Just like time and energy are resources, so are things like currency and support. When certain employees are paid less for doing the same job as their peers—a situation that people from nondominant and marginalized communities know especially well—how can they feel valued and respected? Pay equity, like many technical diversity, equity, and inclusion issues, is directly related to whether people feel they belong. Similarly, if every time I ask for people to help on a project or contribute to an assignment, it's deprioritized, but I see that that isn't the case for my teammates, I will also find belonging harder to achieve. In this way, the belonging competency of resources is not only about whether I have *enough resources* but also about whether *resources are equitably distributed.*

Reciprocity is directly related to relationships and resources, though it's a continuous process. If relationships are the "who" and resources are the "what" in the belonging equation, then reciprocity is the "how." Reciprocity means that within the ecosystem of your team, everyone is engaged in mutual give-and-take. Don't confuse reciprocity with transactions—part of why reciprocity is so hard to achieve is because it *isn't* a perfect one-to-one exchange. When our dynamic is truly reciprocal, I do not help you only because you helped me, just as I won't refrain from helping you if you've never helped me. Reciprocity involves being responsive to the needs of others, monitoring their needs *and* your own, asking for support when your needs emerge, and making sure you have established enough open communication and earned enough trust to continuously loop through this cycle.

A truly healthy team will experience a nonlinear form of reciprocity, one where the idea of "paying it forward" is a given. One employee takes on extra responsibility when their teammate's parent is unexpectedly in need of temporary full-time care; when that employee is anxious about presenting in a leadership meeting alone, *another* team member immediately volunteers to be there. As you consider a scenario like this one, you might ask: "Isn't this just how teams are supposed to work?" Competition for resources, mistrust among teammates or a lack of safety in asking for help, rewarding individual achievement over team success, and unclear roles and responsibilities get in the way of this level of exchange. This is true even on teams where culture and DEI have been major priorities for years.

Take mine, for example. While conducting a quarterly review with one of the leaders on my team, I commented on her absolutely stellar year so far. She had achieved all of her milestones, supported every other team member on her team, and developed a plethora of new skills. In three years with the organization, I had never seen such an exceptional level of performance from her. Still, there was one area where I saw a need for improvement: collaboration. This feedback surprised her. Hadn't this been her most collaborative quarter yet? Hadn't she worked with every single person in the company on something? Both things were true. And yet, in their reviews, two of her teammates had noted that they felt they were "takers" in their relationship with her. They wanted to help take things off her plate, advocate for and support her, and just be what they called "good colleagues" to her. When they tried to help, though, they were often met with a polite "No, thank you." This was making them feel like they were taking advantage of her, not contributing, and taking part in what I call 80/20 relationships: she was giving them 80 percent, but only accepting 20 percent back. To feel a sense of belonging on their team, these two employees wanted to feel they were meeting her needs. When I shared this context with her, she expressed surprise. "It never occurred to me that there should be give-and-take. I was hired in a support role; I've never worked here and had a team of people that were designated to support me back."

In this case, a lack of role clarity—specifically, what role this leader was meant to play with her peers—affected reciprocity. As a manager, it was my responsibility to reset expectations and affirm that her needs could and should be met by others. It was also up to me to map out what that might look like in practice, especially since this leader couldn't conjure up an image of a lateral relationship where she was receiving help.

INCLUSIVE MANAGEMENT TIP THREE:
PRACTICE SELF-REFLECTION

One simple exercise that can help you create a culture of belonging is to reflect on a time you were part of a team—whether professionally, through volunteering, or other group activities—and list out the specific behaviors that helped you feel like you belonged there. How did you know you belonged? What feelings did you experience? Similarly, reflect on a time when you felt you *didn't* belong. What was communicated in that situation, implicitly or explicitly, that triggered this feeling? With this data in mind, consider how you might adopt or eliminate practices on your own team to maximize a sense of belonging. Before you introduce them, invite your teammates to do the same exercise. Together, determine what practices to adopt or attempt.

CONFLICT IN BELONGING NEEDS

So far, we've explored a general view of belonging that applies to most team-wide situations. But what do you do when there is a conflict in belonging needs? Who gets priority? And what is your role in deciding what to do?

First, let's start with what Sharehold and Sarah Judd Welch deem the four types of belonging—foundational, self, group, and societal—in their study "Redesigning Belonging."

Foundational belonging refers to the inherent belief that everyone has a shared humanity that should be honored. While the idea of complete interconnection might be hard to wrap your mind around at first, reflecting on a fundamental loving-kindness meditation technique can help make it more concrete. In loving-kindness, one common visualization practice is to imagine the entire world and every person in it and wish them love, care, and freedom from suffering. You then direct this same feeling of heartfelt goodwill toward yourself. This practice helps you feel foundational belonging in real time! At work, foundational belonging involves the deep-rooted acceptance that your teammates are humans first, workers second.[2]

Self-belonging is the feeling of connection to ourselves. I like to call this type of belonging the "Brené Brown" flavor of belonging because her work on authenticity, vulnerability, and accepting the gifts of imperfection helps people experience self-belonging. When we experience self-belonging, we know that we are inherently worthy and valuable, regardless of what others say about us. Employees who rate themselves high in self-belonging are able to understand how their roles contribute to the larger mission of the organization. They also value their contributions to their teams, even if they don't receive external praise or rewards.

Group belonging is the kind of belonging that managers are most expected to cultivate on their teams. It refers to the experience of feeling part of and accepted in a community, one where reciprocity is natural, contributions are externally recognized, and employees can just "be" together and feel at ease. Employees who experience high rates of group belonging know that if they need help, their peers will pitch in without hesitation.

Societal belonging occurs when people feel that society's structures and codes affirm them. It refers to how we are or aren't accepted in our society and culture, which is usually clear through the ways economic, public safety, public health, housing, criminal justice, and government forces act on us. Since the COVID-19 pandemic and the murder of George Floyd, societal belonging has shown up as a need more regularly at work. As current events and social change affect employees, especially those who have been negatively affected, their desire for organizational affirmation may increase. Think about it. If my society isn't built for me or does not honor my humanity, I might go to the next biggest group I am part of for affirmation and support. Keep this idea in mind when employees ask you to make statements about social justice, natural disasters, or other society-wide events. They may need this from the organization because it's the only group with some power, including to make change, to which they belong.

Because each one of your team members is unique, their current and ideal belonging states will also be unique. Most of the time, this difference will contribute to richness and depth on your team. Sometimes, though, these differences will create conflict.

For example, an employee who highly values and needs self-belonging may bristle when other employees expect behaviors tied to group or foundational belonging. "Why do you need my validation?" they might ask a colleague, who could interpret their response as critical or demeaning. You may have an employee who identifies as having one or more dominant social identities, inherently experiences a high sense of societal belonging, and most values foundational belonging. When their teammate, who is part of a marginalized or historically resilient group that has recently been negatively affected by a current event, asks for public acknowledgment and a pledge from the company to do better, they might take issue. Just like that, they make a statement in opposition to the tune of "We are all human. All humans matter." Now the employee experiencing low societal belonging may experience a drop in their sense of group belonging, not to mention feel disregarded and silenced.

If you are managing employees from different generations, you may see even more of these conflicts since what they were taught to expect from work is different. Baby boomers and millennials, for example, both desire respect from their peers at work (group and foundational belonging), but what respect means to them is different. For example, many baby boomers value hierarchy and job titles, while millennials care more about their personal growth and rapid career progression. Naturally, these are generalizations, and individuals from different generational cohorts may not share the same values as described. The point is that differences in opinion about the value of chain of command and paying dues going from an interpersonal issue to a fundamental question about how *matters* on your team!

Before such conflicts arise, guide your employees through Sharehold's "Redesigning Belonging" report and self-assessment. The self-assessment will help employees understand what their current belonging states are across the four types of belonging. Then, they can think with the rest of the team about what might need to happen for everyone to achieve their ideal states, both inside of and outside of work.

If you find yourself already in a conflict stemming from belonging needs, you have a few different responsibilities. For one, it's up to you to mediate the conflict and help your employees find a common ground or shared goal. You are also charged with ensuring that the conflict stays healthy, meaning that what is discussed are behaviors rather than the employees' characters or belief systems. If the conflict devolves into mean-spirited personal attacks, you must remove your employees from the situation, create a space for cooling down, and resume the conversation with strong ground rules in place.

BELONGING ACTION PLAN

When the people on our teams come from the same backgrounds, perspectives, and identities, belonging is usually an unconscious experience that feels natural and organic. On teams where there are differences, that isn't the case. Belonging is something that has to be actively cultivated and maintained, especially because people's experiences of what belonging is, how much of it they have across the four types, and where they need to see the biggest investments in the Three Rs will differ.

The good news is that, as the team's manager, you have the ability to go directly to the source to understand expectations, experiences, and ideals, and then . . . do something about what you learn! Putting together a **Belonging Action Plan**, a tool and tracker for setting up regular team behaviors to foster belonging, does not have to be an overly complex task. Using what you've learned in this section, ask your employees a few simple questions.

1. Do you feel a sense of belonging on the team?
2. Why or why not?
3. What would increase your sense of belonging on the team?
4. What would you be willing to contribute to increasing other people's sense of belonging?

If you took the Sharehold belonging self-assessment together or have faced conflicts in belonging needs already, be sure to integrate what you learned into your research, as well.

Once you have gathered enough data to start making decisions, chart out what you learned in a table like the one below.

BELONGING COMPETENCY	OPPORTUNITY	PRACTICE	TIMELINE
Relationships			
Resources			
Reciprocity			

Here is an example table codeveloped by a fundraising team at a national nonprofit.

BELONGING COMPETENCY	OPPORTUNITY	PRACTICE	TIMELINE
Relationships	Employees have never met one another in person. They think meeting, even informally, would increase their sense of being in a community.	Plan a team off-site event that brings everyone together at our national headquarters. Recommend some optional social activities to do after working sessions.	Q3
Resources	Employees do not understand why their job descriptions and the pay rates listed in them are different, even though their titles are the same.	Collaborate with human resources to audit and update job descriptions, review pay bands, and discuss the results with team members.	Q4
Reciprocity	Employees often feel overloaded when their colleagues take time off because they do not know what they will need to take on or where to find the resources to complete these unfamiliar tasks.	Collaborate with team members to create a Delegation Tracker, a simple template for employees to fill out before they take time off that lists the task, the delegate, and links to relevant information.	Immediate; complete before the end of the month.

12

PAY EQUITY[1]

AS WE'VE SEEN IN OUR DISCUSSION of the importance of having enough resources to enable a sense of belonging, it's impossible to think about workplace belonging without considering how much people make. In recent years, the laws around pay transparency in the US have quickly changed as a result of employee and state pressures. At the time of this writing, states like California, Colorado, Connecticut, Nevada, and Washington have passed laws requiring employers to include salary ranges in job postings, with more following their examples.

The change, which has been driven by people in underrepresented or nondominant groups demanding fair pay, presents both major opportunities and challenges for employers. Laws and industry standards around publishing pay ranges in job descriptions don't account for the overall impact these changes have on current employees, nor do they consider the ways in which employers may use incentives to keep their existing inequitable practices in place.

For managers hoping to capitalize on this shift as a push toward equity, however, strong change-management practices and a larger equity-based pay strategy may provide the transformation both they and their employees want.

DEFINING AND
COMMUNICATING PAY EQUITY

Pay transparency and pay equity are not the same. **Pay transparency** is simply publishing publicly what the pay is. Even that process may involve publishing only salary ranges on job descriptions, publishing pay bands inside of the organization, or publicly listing out all compensation. You are free to publish pay ranges that are unequal or inequitable, just as you are free to offer signing bonuses or other onetime bonuses to some candidates and not others.

Pay equity, though, is something else entirely. Equity itself is the combination of equal access—to resources and opportunities— and the meeting of individual needs created by cumulative disadvantages. In its simplest form, **equal pay** means paying the same salary to people performing the same role. Equitable pay does not have a uniform definition.

It's up to your organization to define what equitable pay is. Generally, it will start with: we pay people the same amount for performing the same role. After that, you may consider adding a multiplier for folks living in more expensive geographies or adjusting pay upward during times of higher inflation.

As a manager, you may or may not have the ability to directly affect pay decisions. You can, however, always influence and advocate for more equitable practices. To do so effectively, consider two questions.

DO I VALUE MY TEAM MEMBERS THE SAME AMOUNT AS THE MARKET DOES?

When we calculate compensation at Ethos, we start with market-based databases, but we don't end there. Often those databases offer generic views of roles or don't include specialized roles or nonstandard titles, which is why we have to audit job descriptions and create composite ones in our databases. Even then, the market values roles based on supply and demand, not necessarily how much value that role produces or how much a company needs someone in that role to succeed.

In nonprofits, for example, field workers are the organization— without them, there are no programs or services. Yet, they often are valued least by the market. For this reason, we often recommend setting a higher bar for pay, such as paying people at the 75th percentile rather than the 50th or below.

WHAT DOES A GOOD LIFE LOOK LIKE?

This question is harder to answer because it's so subjective. At the same time, it's one of the most vital questions leaders in an organization can address. Equal pay just means parity; it doesn't guarantee a living wage. It certainly doesn't guarantee a living wage for caregivers who are the sole earners in their households. When considering equitable pay, it's worth talking to your employees about what a good life looks like to them. The answers might be more tied to total compensation, specifically benefits like paid sick time and leave time, than base pay. Or they might advocate for higher base pay.

When considering both questions, it's up to you to know your budget and finances well enough to communicate what is and is not possible. You may even create a compensation philosophy specific to your team that any employee can understand, detailing how you make pay decisions, when they are made, and how they are affected.

EDUCATING TEAM MEMBERS

One of the problems with pay transparency without equity is that employees have different exposure to information about pay, not only within your organization but over the course of their lives. Many employees won't have seen a profit and loss statement, cash flow analysis, or annual budget. They may not understand corporate governance and how boards may affect where funds are allocated.

Pay equity is about understanding that everyone deserves to receive the same information and that they may have different needs in how that information is shared and explained. As part of any pay transparency change-management process, every employee should understand:

- how the business makes money;
- what the business expenses are;
- what rules or restrictions are in place around how money is used;
- what percentage of expenses are made up of employee pay;
- how much of employee pay is not captured in base pay (for example, benefits); and
- what the organization's next annual budgeting process will look like.

While your finance and human resources teams might focus on compiling and presenting this information, *you* must be able to answer these questions succinctly and correctly since you will face the most questions from staff. If you find that in the process of answering these questions, you are missing answers or some of those answers are insufficient, this is something to flag as an area of improvement, which you can communicate to your own team members and your leaders. As long as your employees have a projected timeline for when the improvement will be made, they are more likely to accept and support the process than if you said nothing at all.

PREPARING TOTAL
COMPENSATION STATEMENTS

When you publish pay ranges on your open jobs, your current employees can see them just as well as prospective employees. This can lead to hurt feelings, lowered employee sentiment, and even departures. Employees need to understand their own pay, how it was decided, how it does or does not differ from pay listed for open roles, and what the future of their pay will look like.

A total compensation statement can help address these key questions in a straightforward and consistent way. They should always be written from the perspective of the employee, and the actual statement should be delivered in an annual meeting where employees discuss the statement and address any questions they may have about it with you. This conversation should not be combined with performance evaluations, where both sides might be incentivized to discuss performance differently in order to negotiate or justify pay decisions. Specifically, an employee might downplay mistakes they have made or areas where they need to improve to justify that they deserve higher pay, just as a budget-restricted manager might emphasize instances of lower performance to avoid discussing a pay increase.

While there are many ways to approach putting together a total compensation statement, each should include a few basic components.

- **The employee's information:** Name, date of statement, anniversary date with the organization, role title, and job description. All can be used as a reference when discussing pay.
- **Summary of total compensation for the current year:** Make sure to define total compensation as base pay and benefits. Then indicate how much their base pay was, along with the value of each benefit, including health, dental, and

vision insurance, education stipends or credits, sponsored meals, paid time off, and other perks. This is best presented as a table that also notes proration based on start date.

- **Summary of total compensation for the next year:** This is the same table but updated to reflect salary or benefits changes in the next year. You may indicate a cost-of-living adjustment, a projected raise or bonus, or some additional benefit that will be offered.
- **Supporting information:** This may include links or direct excerpts of offer letters, employee handbook policies, or benefits summaries that employees can review in addition to their summary tables.

Ultimately, the total compensation statement is a tailored snapshot of a current employee's pay. This artifact helps them understand where they fall in the organization and demystifies how you arrive at the pay now being published on job boards, which should lead to a smoother change-management process. For a total compensation template you can use with your teammates, visit alidamirandawolff.com/bookreaders.

13

NAVIGATING DIFFERENT ENVIRONMENTS

A HUGE PART OF CREATING THE CONDITIONS for belonging is understanding how to shape and navigate different social environments. How we interact in an office, in remote settings, and even in hybrid workplaces determines the strength and durability of our relationships. Developing a sensitivity to context, regarding not only *where* we are but *who* is there and *how* they are showing up, is also crucial to the success of our teams.

ACCESSIBILITY

According to the Centers for Disease Control and Prevention, as of 2023, sixty-one million people have disabilities in the United States. Globally, people with disabilities are referred to as the largest minority group, with the World Health Organization estimating 1.3 billion people have disabilities, representing 16 percent of the world population. Many researchers in the space of disability consider this to be an underestimate based on challenges in data collection across countries.

This data is especially important to you because at some point you are likely to manage employees with disabilities. In fact, since some studies show that only 4 percent of employees[1] with disabilities disclose those disabilities, you may already be managing folks with disabilities without knowing it.

The reality is that our work environments are typically built for people without disabilities, making the experience for people with disabilities especially challenging. For example, employees who are hard of hearing or Deaf often have to participate in meetings without an interpreter or closed captioning, forcing them to lip-read, or for those who do not lip-read, to use their own assistive technologies or even miss out on the conversation altogether. Not only does this negatively affect their performance and productivity, it also creates a culture of exclusion.

I remember interviewing for a role at a media and advertising firm known for its inclusive culture and people-first ethos. While applying for the role, I kept thinking how lucky I would be to work at a place as progressive and human centered. Between the time I applied and when I received an interview callback, I was hit by a car while crossing the street. I acquired a mobility disability. I required various assistive technologies during that time, like walking aids and access to an iPad with a smart keyboard since I could not grip a pen or pencil. But I was still eager to pursue this job opportunity. I accepted the interview slot and then let them know about the aids I would need to use. Almost immediately, I received a message from the hiring manager explaining that their office building was not accessible and that it would be nearly impossible for me to enter their space. They offered a videoconferencing alternative, which at first seemed like a great compromise. That was, however, until I got into the interview, where no one on the team quite knew how to operate the conferencing software. Needless to say, despite my best efforts, the interview ended up being awkward and short.

How many organizations miss out on exceptionally talented, hardworking people because they don't even consider accessibility?

Managers have the power to make changes to their hiring processes and experiences to mitigate some of the inherently ableist structures in our work environments.

While this is by no means a comprehensive list, here are some practices you can adopt as your "defaults" to promote accessibility.

WRITING JOB DESCRIPTIONS

When writing job descriptions, make sure to include a section about the physical requirements of the role. This may already be a standard practice within your organization, in which case you can collaborate with your leadership or human resources teams on determining which physical responsibilities truly are necessary to do the role. If this isn't a practice, draw from the following examples. As you review them, you might identify other physical requirements necessary to perform the role. Add those in too!

- Must be able to remain in a stationary position 50 percent of the time.
- Must be able to ascend and descend ladders, scaffolds, and stairs and work in confined spaces and in proximity to loud equipment.
- Must be able to frequently move boxes weighing up to 25/50/80 pounds across the facility.
- Must be able to respond quickly to sounds.
- Must be able to move safely over uneven terrain or in confined spaces.
- Must be able to work in cold environments and on concrete floors.
- Must be able to physically navigate small spaces and work around others including sitting, standing, running, and climbing stairs.

OFFERING REASONABLE ACCOMMODATIONS

Organizations headquartered in the US that have fifteen or more employees are generally required to comply with Equal Employment

Opportunity laws. To be Equal Employment Opportunity Employers, they pledge not to discriminate against employees based on race, color, religion, sex, national origin, age, disability, or genetic information. While these laws apply to all work situations, they are most often cited when employers fail to make **reasonable accommodations**. More often than not, the people fulfilling these accommodations are managers.

While some employees with disabilities may clearly understand what reasonable accommodations are and come prepared with their requests, many will not. To create a culture of belonging, it's up to you to proactively share a clear definition along with examples of what accommodations employees may ask you to honor.

Reasonable accommodations are not limited to disability—they can be tied to religious affiliation, culture, or other identities protected by the Equal Employment Opportunity Commission (which are collectively referred to as "the protected classes"). But when it comes to disability, a reasonable accommodation in the workplace allows an employee to perform the essential functions of the job, as long as it does not create undue hardship for the organization. For a qualified individual that has notified the company of their disability, the organization will provide reasonable accommodations under the Americans with Disabilities Act or corresponding state and local laws.

Some commonly requested reasonable accommodations by disability type are represented in the table that follows. Note that these primarily relate to meeting environments.

DISABILITY TYPE	EXAMPLE ACCOMMODATIONS
SPEECH	• Provide alternative ways of communicating (writing, demonstrations, and so on). • Provide text-to-speech assistive technologies. • Set meeting norms with team members to allow for pauses and breaks between verbal exchanges to allow nonspeaking participants to contribute in other forms.

DISABILITY TYPE	EXAMPLE ACCOMMODATIONS
HEARING	• Provide brief notes in writing for any information conveyed auditorily. • Provide interpreter, transcription, and/or captioning services.
NEURODIVERSITY	• Control lights, sounds, and scents. • Provide alternative ways of communicating (writing, demonstrations, and so on).
VISION	• If there are any written documents during meetings, presentations, or other demonstrations, provide alternate options (large print, Braille, electronic, tape-recorded, and so on). • Provide verbal instructions.
MOBILITY	• Provide directions to elevators, ramps, parking, and restrooms for any new space with which employees interact. • Allow people to keep mobility aids nearby. • Prepare space for mobility aids in physical locations and an alternative seating arrangement if they would like to transfer out of their aids. • Offer technology and home office setup tools that account for various forms of mobility disabilities, such as modified keyboards, mice, monitors, chairs, and other supplies necessary for conducting work.
ADDITIONAL	• Allow attendants or support people to attend meetings or team functions when necessary for the employee to participate. • Allow participants to disclose their preferred working time. • Offer assistive communication devices or agree to use devices provided by the employees. • Plan for longer meeting times if requested or needed.

ONBOARDING TEAM MEMBERS

Managers often ask when to bring up reasonable accommodations, if at all. One easy opportunity is to include a review of accommodations directly into the onboarding process. By adopting this practice, you will establish that you and your team are committed to accessibility and inclusivity, which may also give new employees the confidence they need to disclose their disabilities and related needs.

Even if you don't think your new employees have disabilities, reviewing accommodations sets the tone for what you expect. Namely, that all team members must honor accessibility requirements and actively participate in making the work environment "work" for everyone.

MANAGING PERFORMANCE

Part of being a manager is getting really clear on what you should and should not expect from your employees. To create a truly inclusive and equitable workplace, that means taking a hard look at how you define "high performance" and whether it is necessary for the business and fair to employees. As Minal Bopaiah explains in her book, *Equity*, how you reward employees based on the time they contribute can get in the way of your equity goals. Managers can fall into the "above and beyond" trap, characterizing top performers as people who electively work longer hours (without taking overtime) and choose not to take their sick time or vacation time. For employees with disabilities, this mindset, whether shared implicitly or explicitly, can lead to serious health consequences.

For example, if an employee needs to keep a fixed, eight-hour day or forty-hour-per-week schedule in order to make it to necessary medical appointments, is it right if they are not considered for a promotion? Even if they produce high-quality work on time and with the resources available? In order to get the promotion, should they risk the consequences of *not going* to their medical appointments? Taken even further, if an otherwise hardworking and competent employee needs to take additional sick time or even a medical leave, does that time away count *against* them when they return, ready to contribute?

You have a responsibility to ask yourself whether the expectations you hold and the decisions you make relative to performance evaluations reflect biases around disability or create barriers to accessibility. You may find in this process that, rather than bias living within you, the structure of your organization generates undue hardships for employees with disabilities. In that case, it's up to you to generate as many mitigating measures within your team as you can while also advocating for organization-wide changes.

INCLUSIVELY DESIGNING DIFFERENT ENVIRONMENTS

Promoting accessibility is one part of a whole constellation of behaviors you must adopt in order to create belonging on your team. Being able to design for and switch between different working environments is another crucial management skill. The reality is that there are more ways of working inside of each organization, postpandemic, than there were before. You may run a team that shares the same four walls every day or one distributed across the world, working out of coffee shops and home offices. Chances are you are managing a team somewhere in between, where sometimes employees are in a physical shared office but not always and certainly not at the same time. In these inconsistent and changing circumstances, how can you still foster a sense of belonging?

One place to start is by considering the neurobiology of friendship. Stay with me here—science journalist Lydia Denworth studies the science of friendship, and in her work, she's found that to develop close, trusting relationships, we need three key elements: proximity, similarity, and reciprocity.

In Denworth's research, proximity means we share time together in person. Interestingly, Denworth found relationships that formed in person but then became long-distance were much more likely to last than those where this was not the case. Similarity means we have something in common that mutually sparks joy or interest. When people grow apart, a lack of shared interests may be a core driver. Finally, reciprocity means much the same as it does in the Three Rs model: we engage in a healthy practice of give-and-take when we have the confidence that our colleagues, friends, partners, or other close contacts will show up when we need them. With these concepts in mind, you can cultivate the conditions for strong bonds and shared trust on your teams, no matter the office setup or working situation.

IN-OFFICE ENVIRONMENTS

It's easy to romanticize prepandemic officing and ignore all of the very real difficulties that come with being on-site all the time. Remote work existed before the pandemic for many reasons, including the lost productivity and lower quality of life caused by commuting, rigid schedules that didn't allow employees to tend to themselves or their care networks, the business limitations of being in just one time zone, insufficient numbers of skilled workers in a given location leading to understaffing, and so, so many others. We also tend to take for granted that just being in the same place is enough to create bonds and belonging. Workplace loneliness has been an issue since some of the first belonging studies started in the 1980s, so the idea that proximity is all we need is flawed.

Of course, in-office environments *can* lead to healthy cultures and strong collegial ties if they are properly tended and nurtured. Much of how you do this will depend on your organization's rules (including the unspoken ones), your team's preferences, and your own management style. But in my experience, there are a few basic practices that strengthen workplace communities inside of an office.

PROXIMITY	SIMILARITY	RECIPROCITY
Make sure all of your collaboration spaces are accessible for all employees.	Don't be afraid of introducing small talk and vibe checks in team meetings; the discovery of shared interests can lead to stronger bonds.	Flexibility is critical to reciprocity; for example, caregivers on the team can show up for their colleagues better if they can adjust their schedules to meet their family needs.
Ensure there are both communal and private spaces so people can both collaborate and take advantage of focus time (think kitchen or cafeteria versus offices or phone booths).	Showcase common goals where your team normally gathers together, such as displaying the number, like the number of happy customers or contracts closed on a mounted screen.	If there are limited resources on the team, like conference rooms, create a sharing schedule to help stave off potential conflicts and reinforce the idea of give-and-take.
Experiment with changing seating assignments to help colleagues who don't work together as often connect over a shared space.	If you find something that team members have in common, like a love of Beyoncé, native plant gardening, or competitive running, integrate related elements into the physical environment, like signs, pictures, or decor.	Start a team library where employees can bring their favorite books and take others their colleagues have brought.
Rethink the concept of office space altogether by organizing meetings over lunch at a café, in a nearby park, or even just on another floor—remember, the key is to be together, not be nailed down to the same seat for eight hours.	Establish an in-person team ritual, like shared meals or early-morning all-team check-ins.	Encourage "Ask for Help" prompts in meetings to facilitate a regular practice of employees raising their hand for help from their colleagues.

REMOTE ENVIRONMENTS

Just as there are challenges with in-office environments, remote workplaces come with their own set of problems. A popular phrase during the quarantine period of 2020 was: "We're not working from home. We're living at work." Depending on where employees work, they may not have a strong sense of separation between their work and home lives. Plus, spending all of their time on screens has psychological and physical consequences, from eye strain to depression, anxiety, and even heart disease caused by a lack of physical movement during the day. Remote workers also report a greater pressure to be constantly online throughout the day to prove they are working hard. Depending on their thinking and processing styles, being alone for extended periods can affect their ability to focus and stay engaged with their work. Finally, remote workers often feel more isolated, have fewer people to turn to for help, and can find that issues outside of their control, like a poor internet connection or the absence of important office equipment like printers, scanners, and fax machines, can affect their performance.

Yet, people from underrepresented, underserved, and historically resilient groups often *prefer* remote work because of the flexible schedules, ability to have control over their environments, and freedom to work in a way that aligns more to their strengths than predetermined in-office decorum can. And creating a sense of belonging across distances *is* possible, so long as there is an underlying structure to the remote work. To make the most of a remote workplace, consider the three elements of close relationships a little differently.

PROXIMITY	SIMILARITY	RECIPROCITY
As much as possible, encourage employees to keep their cameras on during one-on-ones and larger meetings.	Schedule "commute time" between virtual meetings so folks can simulate the experience of catching up on the way to the break room without the fear of missing another meeting.	Set clear guidelines for when people are expected to be online and when they are not; keep time zones in mind when you do.
Work with your organizational leaders to set up formal or informal in-person meetups between team members at set times during the year.	Introduce asynchronous prompts into your communication tools tied to hobbies, interests, hopes, and plans.	Start an #AskForHelp channel on your internal company messaging platform where team members can post problems and solutions.

PROXIMITY	SIMILARITY	RECIPROCITY
If your work function requires travel, send team members to conferences, customer sites, or other offices together in small groups.	Remote teams can become siloed quickly; when one team member brings an idea or problem to you, connect them with another team member going through something similar.	Encourage team members to practice digital coworking, where a videoconference simulates the experience of working next to each other and occasionally asking a question or sharing a resource.
Leave room for unstructured time, rather than back-to-back meetings, so employees can call one another, send chat messages, or just take five minutes to check in with one another,	Invest in building a common language, including making a glossary out of all of the terms and phrases your teammates use on a regular basis.	Encourage "Ask Me Anything" meetings where a team member can troubleshoot problems related to their role with anyone else on the team who needs help.

HYBRID ENVIRONMENTS

Hybrid environments may seem appealing as a middle option, but they present their own challenges precisely because they are "in between." Communication breakdowns happen between in-office and remote employees. Missed meetings and calendaring mix-ups abound whenever someone switches time zones. Neither the in-office or remote work environments are set up to accommodate the other, meaning people feel left out, ignored, or deprioritized.

Many of the practices in both the in-office and remote sections will be useful for hybrid teams but only if adapted to accommodate the specific challenges of cross-communication and collaboration when people are using different tools and approaches.

For example, when leading team meetings, it's important in hybrid settings to make sure a 360-degree camera is available so everyone joining remotely can see the people in the room. On the flip side, those joining remotely should keep their cameras on. Prep beforehand may be necessary to make sure everyone is audible and coming across clearly. You may want to turn on auto-captions and test them to make sure they work for all people attending the meeting. You will also want to make sure you have a designated meeting lead to regularly check the chat for written communication and course correct when sidebar conversations start in the office conference room. Similarly, this person may set a rule that every person must have a chance to share during the meeting, regularly pausing and evaluating to create the space for everyone to speak.

When facilitating training or learning events in a live format with people joining in person and remotely, ensure that you have two facilitators: one in the room leading exercises, and one in the virtual setting doing the same. These facilitators will present the material together but answer questions, guide exercises, and navigate breakouts for the specific spaces they are in—virtual or in person. This setup ensures one group isn't favored or prioritized over another.

INCLUSIVE MANAGEMENT TIP FOUR: BECOME THE TEST CASE

There's nothing like firsthand experience to help illuminate the benefits and drawbacks of a particular experience. As you design work environments for your team members, start by testing out your ideas on yourself. For example, if you want to try out a new interactive polling tool for the next all-team meeting, start by using it in a smaller test environment. Ask yourself: "Does this add to the experience, like adding in a gaming component to the conversation? Or does it create unforeseen consequences, such as redirecting me out of my videoconferencing app and away from people's faces?" While this may seem like basic advice, remember that the temptation to just do things without trying them out first will be strong as you manage competing priorities. But managers who take the time to develop their ideas before implementing them are much more likely to have credibility with their team members and facilitate better experiences.

14

EQUITABLE GOAL SETTING[1]

FOR MANY PEOPLE, PRODUCTIVITY MEANS PROGRESS. In popular business-speak, it could as easily be defined as "bigger" and "more." At least, that's what Dismantling Racism Works and the Centre for Community Organizations argue in their DEIB white paper, "White Supremacy Culture in Organizations." Through their analysis, they determined that progress is not inherently negative or white supremacist. Rather, when progress is "understood as organizational expansion (i.e., adding staff or projects) or the ability to serve more people, regardless of how well the community is being served," it runs the risk of creating exclusion, burnout, and organizational failure, with the most severe consequences happening along racial lines. Naturally, all of these effects get in the way of cultivating a genuine culture of belonging where everyone feels valued and respected.

For example, if your pursuit of rapid growth leads to increased staff injuries or an 8 percent reduction of your workforce during a period of high inflation, creating serious setbacks for your former employees, a "bigger" and "more" approach might actually work *against* advancement and achievement. As a manager, you have an ethical responsibility to your employees. If you "move fast and break things" when it comes to employees, what ends up broken is people, and most likely, those already facing the greatest disadvantages. That's why being an inclusive and equitable manager means being intentional about how you define productivity, progress, and goals with your various team members.

So, how do you coach your employees to pursue goals that are both ambitious and manageable? How do you balance the very real need for creativity, innovation, and momentum with the equally valid need of creating stability, security, and safety?

Start by asking long-term vision-related questions. In any goal-setting exercise, aligning to a greater vision keeps the goals from being distractions or detractors and, instead, helps set a clear focus. Some questions to ask yourself as you enter quarterly and annual goal-setting cycles are:

- Why do we want to grow?
- What do we gain by growing?
- What do we lose or give up by growing?
- What does growth mean this year? Next year? In five years?
- How will our team members be affected by growth?
- Will some team members benefit more from the company's growth than others? Why or why not?
- How can we maintain what we have that matters (for example, our strong customer relationships, our team's well-being, our product or service quality) as we grow?

As part of your goal-setting exercises, make sure to create room to celebrate the process as a means of reaching progress. Despite the popularity of phrases like, "It's not the destination, it's the journey," our business goals tend to focus primarily on outcomes. The same applies to performance goals. Don't just focus on the fact that an employee met their sales quota, which should be celebrated, but also how they met it. There's a big difference between meeting the quota while cutting corners, edging in on colleagues' deals, or overpromising what other teams can't deliver and meeting that quota with honesty, integrity, and groundedness.

Finally, remember to set thoughtful, high-minded goals even in lean times. Too often when managers set goals around costs, the focus is only on *financial costs*. But what about the other costs? What will this cost us in terms of our culture? Our working environment? Our values? Our other limited resources, like time, energy, and morale?

Risk exists beyond financial loss, and it's worth broaching the subject of what folks stand to lose beyond dollars. On the flip side, rewards come in many forms, not just revenue, profit, and incentive pay. When asking what success would look like, invite folks to think about whether it would mean their full team stays together (low to no turnover), employees report feeling a sense of belonging in the organization (positive sentiment), or customers rate their experiences with the organization more highly (customer satisfaction). It's also worth asking employees what a reward means to them; at one organization we recently surveyed, employees elected for more paid time off and sick leave instead of cash bonuses.

PART THREE

INCLUSIVE LANGUAGE

IN PART ONE, we identified what it means to be a manager-ally. One of the stark realities of taking on that role is that you will have to navigate tough conversations, especially about identity. Many times, you may feel unequipped for these conversations and question whether saying nothing at all is the best approach. Don't succumb to this fear! It's better to make a mistake, apologize, learn, and grow than to say nothing and stay stuck. The truth is, you will say the wrong thing . . . at least once. Creating a culture of belonging and being an inclusive manager requires risk.

15

THE SOCIAL IDENTITIES

A SOCIAL IDENTITY IS ONE YOU HOLD because you belong physically, mentally, and emotionally to a broader social group. Your social identity is directly tied to whether others see you as part of that social group. This is why you so often hear about the distinction between visible and invisible identities.

If your social identity is visible, you will likely be labeled whether you strongly feel part of that social group or not. I, for example, look like I am a millennial and I *am* a millennial. My age is a visible identity. Even though I don't strongly identify with the social group of millennials, assumptions are made about me based on this perceived group membership.

With invisible identity, you will not be labeled unless you or someone else discloses that identity. My chronic illnesses are not observable, which makes my disability status invisible.

The most common social identities that will show up in your day-to-day management of your employees are:

- age
- body type/size
- caregiver status
- disability
- education level

- gender identity
- national origin / nationality
- race / ethnicity
- religion
- sexuality / sexual orientation
- socioeconomic status
- tribal / indigenous affiliation

Increasingly, political affiliation comes up as a "thirteenth" identity. There is debate in the DEI community about whether political affiliation is a social identity. While I did not consider the category a social identity in my first book, *Cultures of Belonging*, I have come to believe that political affiliation *is* a social identity.

Specifically, our different political ideologies form the basis of social groups, and people both strongly identify with or are strongly identified by them. This holds true even when we don't have a political affiliation or ideology at all, since we would then be part of the apolitical social group. Besides, politics comes up at work all the time. When political discussions or issues arise, you will be expected as the team leader to respond. Understanding what to say, and what not to say, is critical to your complex new role.

16

INCLUSIVE LANGUAGE
BEST PRACTICES

EVEN IF YOU AREN'T SURE YOU CAN RETAIN all of the key identity groups or terms, committing a few inclusive language principles to memory will help you enormously as you pursue your inclusive management journey. Remember, the reason inclusive language matters has nothing to do with what the PC police think, and everything to do with showing your colleagues the care and respect they deserve.

CHOOSE INTENTION ABOVE EASE

We often use exclusive or biased language unintentionally. Even though it might feel easier to use idioms or language shorthand, this strategy often perpetuates microaggressions. Ask yourself this: What's more important—being able to speak before you think or the impact your words have on others?

Try to be precise about the words you use that describe identities. If you mean "humans," say "humans" instead of "mankind," which can exclude anyone who doesn't identify as a man. The same applies when you talk about people in terms of occupation.

"Firefighter" is a better choice than "fireman," just as "business-person" is better than "businessman." Similarly, when describing someone's ethnicity or nationality, refer to the specific nation, people, or ethnic group. "Enrolled in the Cowlitz tribe" is much more accurate and often more affirming than "Native American." Many people who are identified as Latine or Asian actually prefer to have their specific country of origin named, such as Mexican American or Filipinx.

Describing someone in terms of what they aren't can also be invalidating and reaffirm a less-than status. This is why describing someone as a person of color is preferable to non-White.

Ask yourself: Is this person's social identity relevant to the conversation? What does using it as a descriptor do? If the individual's identity isn't relevant, don't include it. For example, saying your plane was captained by a female pilot may reinforce the stereotype that being a female pilot is unusual or outside the norm. Saying Amelia Earhart was the first female pilot to fly solo across the Atlantic Ocean, however, is relevant.

HONOR THE PLATINUM RULE

The best way to avoid saying the wrong thing is to create the space for people to tell you how they want to be described. This idea aligns with my favorite DEI rule, the **Platinum Rule**, which says treat others how *they* want to be treated. The Platinum Rule is one of the reasons naming pronouns is so important in new contexts.

For example, if you don't know how a person identifies and can't find out for whatever reason, stick to identity-neutral language, such as using "they" instead of gendered pronouns. But what about the argument that using a plural pronoun for an individual person is grammatically incorrect? First of all, it's worth interrogating why placing the use of normative language (he/she pronouns) above respecting and honoring transgender people with inclusive terms (they/them) is a default. Second, for those linguistics nerds reading this book, consider that language is ever-changing and malleable, with the so-called rules often changing with generations. If we're willing to add words like "selfie" and "meme" to our official dictionaries, why aren't we willing to make adjustments to pronoun usage for the people who need them? Language exists, after all, to meet human needs; humans don't exist to meet the needs of a construct they created!

SAY NO TO CULTURAL CLICHÉS AND IDIOMS

It's a running joke in my organization that for a team of people who collectively have no interest in team sports, we use baseball metaphors constantly. "You knocked it out of the park" and "you threw me a curveball" are two examples. This is because baseball-speak, with all of its connotations of masculinity and Americana, has become ingrained in business culture. It's not only exclusionary to people who don't count English as their native language but also to anyone historically left out of baseball, which is a lot of people.

This same logic applies to any specialized language that might leave people out, whether in their ability to comprehend what you are saying (that is, acronyms and jargon) or whom the language conjures (that is, cultural clichés).

DON'T CHOCK THINGS UP TO "COMMON SENSE"

At least once a month, a manager I am teaching or coaching tells me that *no one* uses the N-word anymore. Let me tell you—they do, *at work*, all the time.

While this is an extreme example, avoiding culturally insensitive language or slurs should not be talked about as a "common sense issue" because sometimes using common sense isn't enough.

In *Dare to Lead*, Brené Brown talks about how, in giving a workshop, she used the word "gypped," and one of the attendees felt personally attacked and excluded. Brown simply did not know that *gypped* is a derogatory term that associates the Roma people, also called gypsies, with cheating and swindling or that this term is often used to describe the Jewish people.

The reality is that many common expressions derive from derogatory terms associated with specific social identities or are adaptations of words with specific and important cultural meanings for the groups that originated them. If you don't know what a word means or where it comes from, look it up! And, you have another choice too—don't use idioms at all. Why not say you felt "cheated" instead of "gypped"? This means you avoid negative associations with different social identity groups, include people who don't know the idioms for language-based and cultural reasons, and generally improve the clarity of your communication in the process.

Here are some examples of common idioms and their more inclusive alternatives.

IDIOM	NEGATIVE CONNOTATION	ALTERNATIVE
GRANDFATHER IN	The grandfather clause is an American historical legal mechanism used to keep Black people after the Civil War from voting by continuing the conditions of antebellum slavery. Using the idiom invokes a history of slavery that continues in many legal and political policies and practices today.	exempt, honor a legacy
GURU	If you are describing a Hindu or Buddhist spiritual guide or leader, the term is appropriate. If you are using the term to describe expertise in an area, rather than its intended usage within the context of Buddhism and Hinduism, it diminishes practitioners or members of these religious groups.	expert, teacher
NINJA	Ninjas were a class of mercenaries in Japanese feudal society. To say someone is a "ninja" at a given trade, like saying someone is an "administrative ninja," appropriates the cultural history of a specific working class of Japanese people, called *shinobi* in the Japanese language.	expert, virtuoso
SHERPA	Sherpa is not an occupation but an ethnic group that refers to eighteen clans in Nepal. By using this term for a general guide, members of the ethnic clan are diminished to the status of "mountain guide" or "porter" and their heritage is erased.	guide, porter
SPIRIT ANIMAL	In some indigenous spiritual and cultural traditions, a spirit animal is a major part of the experience. To refer to Britney Spears or Grumpy Cat as your spirit animal trivializes an entire system of belief.	kindred spirit

INCLUSIVE MANAGEMENT TIP FIVE:
START BY ASKING

When in doubt, start by asking your employees how they identify and why. Make sure to give them a clear "opt-out" if they don't want to engage in the discussion, and help prepare them for the experience by naming your own identities, at least the ones that matter to you most. Why the need to opt out? Depending on the circumstances, place, and time, it may not be safe or desirable to name these identities. The last thing you want is to force an employee to "out" themselves as an identity they are choosing to cover or conceal for safety reasons. As the legislative environment in the United States evolves to severely restrict the rights of trans people, for example, pronoun usage might actually put some of your employees at risk.

17

THE SOCIAL IDENTITY TYPES

BY NOW, YOU MIGHT BE THINKING there are a lot of *rules* to inclusive language. The reality is that once you learn some of the key principles and language alternatives, adopting alternatives is second nature.

And it's no different from the ways we adopt language based on contextual needs. We simplify the words we use when we talk to young children, just as we expect their teachers not to use curse words with them. We often avoid using what our parents would call "disrespectful" or "coarse" language when around our elders. I've noticed the latter on a number of occasions when I've observed my good friend, who also happens to be an anarchist with a penchant for swearing, say "Yes, ma'am" and "No, sir."

If you don't memorize the language in this section, that's okay! It's here as a guide and a reference to help you feel supported when you're afraid of saying the wrong thing.

AGE

Age refers to how old you are and your generation. So, if you are twenty-five, you would be considered "young," in the "twenty-five-to-thirty-four demographic," and "Gen Z." Age is an interesting category because, provided you live a long life, you will move in and out of the dominant and nondominant categories. Remember, for our purposes, "dominant" means in power and "nondominant" means subject to that power. Some practitioners view the ages of twenty-five to forty-four to be dominant based on how advertisers cater to this group, while others look to government officials as a marker, where in the US senators are an average of sixty-one years old. Regardless, when discussing age, keep a few ideas in mind.

- When using gendered age terms, ensure they're age appropriate. "Girl" refers to someone under the age of eighteen and "woman" over the age of eighteen, for example.
- Avoid age terms unless relevant to the content. Most of the time, the phrase "for your age" in the workplace will be an indicator that you might be veering into microaggression territory. Saying, "You're an excellent marketer" and "you're an excellent marketer *for your age*" mean different things. In the former, you are very good in your function. In the second, the implication is that, because of your age, the bar was set lower and less was expected from you. The same goes for, "You are a tech whiz!" and "For your age, you are a tech whiz!"
- Avoid negative connotations or pathologizing language around aging; instead, use neutral or normalizing language. Avoid *othering* language, such as *the elderly, seniors,* and *aging dependents*. Instead, use factual language, such as *older adults*.

BODY TYPE AND SIZE

Body type and size refers to the physical characteristics of your body, including weight, height, and shape. One way to consider body type and size is to consider built environments and ask, "Was this space built for me?" If you are navigating in-person spaces or even helping employees set up their home offices, you will likely encounter, implicitly or explicitly, situations where the fact that people have bodies matters. From team members whose legs don't touch the ground when seated to those who just can't reach the office supplies cabinets, the experience of navigating inaccessible spaces is almost a given in our modern workplaces.

This is especially true when we consider weight. According to Harvard University's School of Health, two out of every three Americans is overweight or obese, and globally, one billion people are expected to be obese by 2030. But our built environments, media images, and societal values around weight do not reflect the state of the majority of people. As bodies grow in size, airplane seats shrink. Recreational use of expensive obesity and diabetes drugs floods our social media feeds and enters our watercooler conversations. Stereotypes about people's intelligence, self-discipline, and reliability on the basis of weight impact who gets promoted and when. Not to mention the very real physical consequences of inaccessible environments for larger-bodied people. In *Hunger*, Roxanne Gay represents in detail the experience of being forced to sit in a chair several sizes too small during a speaking event—a regular occurrence—and the excruciating pain of having the arms and legs dig into her flesh, leaving bruises and welts that lasted well beyond the program.

When talking about body type and size,

- avoid language that promotes body consciousness, body shaming, and the importance of appearances;
- avoid making value judgments about healthy or unhealthy diets;
- avoid using terms like "ugly," "deformed," "weird looking," or others that comment negatively on the appearance of a person or a body part; and
- use body-neutral language, which supports a belief that your body *as it is* deserves acceptance.

EXCLUSIVE LANGUAGE	INCLUSIVE ALTERNATIVE
overweight, obese	larger bodies, people of size
weight loss	lifestyle change
normal height	average height
fat chance	no chance
clean up nicely	look nice; look polished

CAREGIVER STATUS

Caregivers are people who take care of dependents without receiving compensation. Most often, people associate caregiving with parenthood, but it refers to any kind of relationship where someone meets the primary needs of others. You may provide care to family members, biological or chosen. In many cultures, women are assigned the role of primary caregivers, though this is not always the case.

Be mindful of your assumptions on who is taking on caregiving responsibilities and who is not. When it comes to parenthood, consider that caregivers may include nonparental figures, divorced parents, incarcerated parents, and foster parents, to name a few. Sticking with this example, qualifying the validity of a caregiver's status perpetuates harmful stereotypes and creates exclusion. For example, referring to someone as a "natural parent" rather than a "biological parent" undermines the role of an adoptive parent.

Since caregiving often comes with gendered connotations, avoiding assumptions is also important when naming partners and describing pregnancy. A woman can be pregnant, but a pregnant person does not have to identify as a woman. This is due in part to the differences between gender and sex, which are detailed more in following sections.

EXCLUSIVE LANGUAGE	INCLUSIVE ALTERNATIVE
pregnant woman	pregnant person, gestational parent
wife or husband	partner, spouse
nonbiological parent/child/relative	parent, child, relative
adopted child, adopted relative	child, relative
surrendered for adoption	placed for adoption
adopted person	person who was adopted
real parent or natural parent	birth parent, biological parent

DISABILITY

Disability, under the Americans with Disabilities Act, refers to whether you experience functional limitations in activities such as walking, talking, seeing, hearing, or learning. I prefer Emily Ladau's definition from *Demystifying Disability*: "To me, disability is quite simply a natural part of the human experience. And so, there is no singular definition that can be used. But at the end of the day, I just describe it as part of what makes someone a human being. And unfortunately, that's not how everybody understands disability because we've been socialized to think about it as this deeply negative and shameful thing."

So many of our phrases associate disability with all that's negative, as opposed to recognizing that much of what we consider disability is a product of our social structures and environments rather than a deficiency in disabled people. Take the word "crazy" for example. To those with mental disabilities, the casual use of the word *crazy* isn't innocuous; it solidifies a social message that people with these disabilities are dangerous, out of control, and unable to care for themselves. What we say, we end up believing.

This is why one of the most important parts of inclusive language when it comes to disability is the use of identity-first and person-first language.

- **Identity-first:** The disability justice movement is credited as the first group to broadly embrace the identity-first language model. It is often used as an expression of cultural pride and a reclamation of a disability or chronic condition that once conferred a negative identity. Over time, more groups have embraced identity-first language. Here are examples of communities with noted identity-first language preferences.

  Autism or Autism Spectrum Disorder: Opinions within the autism advocacy community vary, but many subgroups advocate for the use of "autistic person" because they view autism as part of an identity, not a condition.

  Deaf or hard of hearing: Many Deaf or Deaf-Blind individuals prefer to be called "hard of hearing," "Deaf," or "Deaf-Blind" (capitalized) rather than "hearing impaired," or "people with hearing loss." This is because Deaf and Deaf-Blind communities are cultures and communities. They are not something you "have" but rather groups you belong to.

  Blind or visually impaired: Members of the blind community may use identity-first terms such as "blind" or "visually impaired person" over people-first terms like "person with blindness."

- **Person-first:** Person-first language is particularly useful when describing someone whose personal history, social identity, or exact medical diagnosis is unfamiliar to you. Person-first language can replace many commonly used descriptors that stigmatize or otherwise convey value judgments about others. Examples of situations in which person-first language is appropriate are listed in the table below.[1]

IDENTITY FIRST	PERSON FIRST
addict	person with a substance use disorder (SUD)
AIDS victim	person with AIDS
alcoholic	person with alcohol use disorder (AUD)
brain damaged	person with a traumatic brain injury
crazy	person with a mental health disorder, person living with a mental health condition (you may either keep the general language or, if given permission, name the specific condition, such as schizophrenia or bipolar disorder)
handicapped person, invalid, cripple	person with a mobility disability, person with a physical disability
special needs, differently abled	person with a mental disability, child with a congenital disability
wheelchair-bound person, confined to a wheelchair	wheelchair user, person using a wheelchair

Unlike other social identities that make people feel hyper visible, disability is an identity where strangers may express open discomfort, embarrassment, and a desire to "not see" the individuals in front of them. So when might you see issues of disability show up among your employees?

We've all seen it—the Instagram post picturing a person with a mobility disability hitting the gym, with a caption like: "What's your excuse?" This response, though well intentioned, is ableist. It suggests that you should be "better than" someone who is

overcoming a disadvantage or "deficiency," when they may disagree with that characterization altogether. To be praised or used
as a measuring stick for those without disabilities is othering. As a
manager, you will want to avoid such othering, especially in situations where you praise a disabled employee for something you
would take for granted with an employee who isn't disabled. For
example, if you wouldn't compliment an employee without a speech
impediment for taking on a public speaking opportunity, then don't
compliment an employee *with* one for doing it, unless you know
for a fact that they saw it as a growth opportunity themselves.

We also want to avoid describing people with disabilities as suffering or struggling, which they may not be. Just because you
imagine yourself struggling with hearing loss does not mean
someone who is hard of hearing experiences themselves as struggling at all. Any kind of language that suggests an employee has a
negative orientation toward or experience of their disability that
isn't backed up by their own statements is more about you than it
is about them. As a new manager, you always want to make sure
your feedback is truly about the employee and not about yourself
or how you might feel if you were them.

Finally, to be truly inclusive, root out phrases that use disabilities as metaphors or trivialize the real consequences of living with
disabilities in a society that makes doing so challenging. Refer to
the table below for better options.

EXCLUSIVE LANGUAGE	INCLUSIVE ALTERNATIVE
all-hands meeting, stand-up meeting	team meeting
crazy, insane	unbelievable, wild, unreal
dumb	frustrating, confusing
following blindly	following aimlessly
lame	bad, awful, boring
tone-deaf	oblivious, not in tune with

EDUCATION LEVEL

How you talk about education level will send a message to your teammates about what you value and who has a chance at development and opportunity in your organization. After all, **education level** and elitism are interconnected. In the US, we tend to associate more education with higher intelligence, class standing, and income. Whether someone completed some high school, graduated from high school, completed some college, graduated from college, began postgraduate studies, or completed an advanced degree is not the only determinant of their professional capabilities, health and well-being, social relationships, or political affiliation.

As much as possible, avoid:

- making negative comments about someone's intelligence or qualifications because of the school they went to or the amount of school they completed;
- associating less education with nondominant races, ethnicities, genders, religious identities, or other identities subject to dominant group power;
- justifying hiring, promotion, or evaluation decisions on the basis of what kind of education someone received or how elite or highly rated the school they attended is; and
- assuming everyone has the same amount of education as you or your own direct leaders.

When we have had relatively easy access to higher education, it can be second nature to assume everyone we work with has too. Yet access to education is a major privilege not afforded to everyone.

A few years ago, I was leading a training for about a hundred people in a technology firm. When trying to illustrate the pervasiveness of elitism in the tech sector, I said, "I bet no one here has ever been denied a job opportunity because of a lack of college education." An employee came to me afterward to explain this had been their experience many times as someone who completed a GED but did not attend college. My statement made her feel both invalidated and singled out.

GENDER IDENTITY AND SEX

Gender, gender identity, sex, and sexual orientation are not the same, but they get conflated constantly. Part of being a manager will involve working with people of many different genders, including ones with which you may be unfamiliar.

The issue of gender identity, in particular, may be especially salient as legislation in several states creates restrictions on gender-affirming care. At the time of this writing, the Movement Advancement Project reported that nineteen states have introduced laws restricting gender-affirming care, including five where providing such care is classified as a felony.[2] You may have to partner with your internal human resources and compliance teams to ensure employees working across different states understand employment resources available to them. For example, with a recent notice of Florida as a "no travel zone" for trans people, you might want to consider what conferences to send employees to or provide guidance on work travel that involves stopovers in the state's airports.

Here's a quick primer.

- **Gender** is a social construct and social identity. It relates to attitudes, feelings, and behaviors a culture associates with an individual's biological sex.
- **Gender identity** describes an individual's psychological sense of their own gender and may or may not correspond with the individual's sex assigned at birth. *Cisgender* means a person's sex assigned at birth corresponds with their gender identity. *Transgender* and *gender nonconforming*

mean a person's gender identity, expression, and/or role are not aligned with what is culturally associated with their sex assigned at birth. Other gender identity terms used by individuals whose sex assigned at birth vary from cultural gender associations include "genderqueer," "gender nonbinary," and "agender."

- **Sex**, which is often broken into the binary of "male" or "female," refers to the assignment a doctor gave a baby upon either looking at their genitalia or conducting a genetic material screening.
- **Sexual orientation** relates to an individual's sexual and emotional attraction, behavior, and/or resulting social affiliation with others.

With all of this in mind, it's important to avoid presuming everyone is cisgender or addressing only cisgender needs. One example of supporting *all* the genders is by using the pronouns with which employees identify themselves.

GENDER	SUBJECTIVE	OBJECTIVE	POSSESSIVE	REFLEXIVE
feminine	she	her	hers	herself
masculine	he	him	his	himself
gender neutral	they	them	theirs	themself
gender neutral	ze	hir/zir	hirs/zirs	hirself/zirself
gender neutral (no pronouns; using a name instead)	[name]	[name]'s	[name]'s	[none; sentence becomes more concise]

When in doubt, use a singular "they" (or "them" or "theirs," as the context requires). This practice helps avoid misgendering a person, which is especially important when interviewing prospective employees or meeting with new folks as you enter new cross-collaborative environments because of your recent promotion into management. In fact, as much as possible, using gender-neutral language promotes inclusion and clarity. Here is a list of examples.

EXCLUSIVE LANGUAGE	INCLUSIVE ALTERNATIVE
chairman	chairperson
clergymen	clergy, clerics
congressman	member of Congress
delivery man, mailman	courier, delivery person
forefathers	ancestors, antecedents
guys (figurative)	folks/team/everyone
headmaster	principal/head of school
man/mankind	people/humanity
man-made	synthetic/manufactured
manpower	personnel/staff
middleman	contact/intermediary/liaison

NATIONAL ORIGIN

National origin can refer to immigration and citizenship, specifically whether you immigrated to the US and are a citizen. Holding citizenship provides benefits and privileges that not holding citizenship does not, including work authorization and the freedom to stay inside the country without fear of detention or deportation. National origin can also tie to cultural identity, such as identifying with the nationality of Italian or Guyanese.

Language that is inclusive of national origin is careful not to assume everyone is a citizen of the United States or identifies as American. Many public services and institutions serve people who are not American citizens, as well as individuals with a wide range of immigration and visa statuses. The most inclusive word choice when referring to the public is dependent on context. "People," "the public," "users," or "folks" are all acceptable alternatives.

EXCLUSIVE LANGUAGE	INCLUSIVE ALTERNATIVE
alien, foreigner, illegal	undocumented person, immigrant
Occidental	Western
Oriental	Asian

RACE/ETHNICITY

Race and ethnicity are separate but related categories. Race refers to a group of people who are viewed as sharing the same physical traits. Ethnicity refers to a group sharing cultural traits, such as the same language or customs. Race, ethnicity, and religion are often all interconnected in someone's self-conception and outside perception. That's why the Platinum Rule is so crucial: always default to asking people how they identify rather than making assumptions.

For example, not all Black people identify as African Americans, with many Black people who live in the United States identifying with Caribbean and African roots rather than American ones. Similarly, some Hispanic people (Spanish-speaking people) identify themselves as Latine or South American, but not all of them do.

While there are many "right" ways to talk about race and ethnicity, there are wrong ones too. For example, the term "Caucasian" has racist origins tied to **phrenology** and **eugenics**, and is inaccurate because it technically refers to people from the Caucasus region of Europe. If you mean White or Irish American, then use those terms.

Race, ethnicity, nationality, and national origin are all connected, which makes specificity important for honoring every person's dignity and sense of self. You may hear people use the terms *Asian* and *Asian American* interchangeably, but they are fundamentally different. An Asian American person has ties to Asia and identifies as American, whereas someone who identifies as Asian may not be an American citizen or, if they are, may simply not identify with that American culture as strongly as an Asian one. Similarly, you may notice your colleagues refer to people as Spanish when they mean Spanish-speaking. A Spanish person is from Spain; however, there are approximately 450 million native Spanish speakers in the world and less than fifty million Spaniards living in Spain, a large proportion of whom speak languages other than Spanish as their primary language, such as Catalan, Galician, Basque, and Aranese.

RELIGION

Religion refers to the system of faith or worship you practice and may include not practicing any system. For reference, the US is home to the largest number of Christians in the world, with 205 million in 2020.

Like socioeconomic status, religion is an identity category that has historically been downplayed within organizations. The dominant religion in the US is Christianity, but it is far from the only religion practiced, so it's important not to impose a Christian lens by default or to the exclusion of other religious identities. But your role as a manager means you will often discuss religion or faith in one way or another, especially as it may relate to paid time off, floating holidays, or cultural observances.

If you're referencing religious observances, don't assume people automatically observe Easter or Christmas, for example, and leave space for non–Judeo-Christian traditions to be discussed, observed, and celebrated. Using religious language out of context may offend people who ascribe to that faith or exclude people who are outside of it. When possible, use alternatives.

EXCLUSIVE LANGUAGE	INCLUSIVE ALTERNATIVE
a blessing in disguise	bad thing that turns out to be good
my mecca / their mecca	special place
fall from grace	lose favor
in limbo	uncertain state
raise hell	cause a disturbance
sacred cow	protected interest, protected subject, unaddressable issue
salt of the earth	worthy and commendable

SEXUAL ORIENTATION

Sexual orientation relates to the gender or gender identity to which a person is physically attracted. Because sexual orientation can be an invisible identity, it's critical not to "out" employees in your descriptions of them. Even if you know their sexual orientation, they may not want it to be known more broadly. Remember, many employees experience inclusion on their teams even as they feel excluded in the larger organization or among their customers. Moreover, if you manage employees distributed across the world, you may encounter tricky situations related to conflicts in company policy versus national policy. For example, many international organizations struggle to establish LGBTQIA2+ affinity groups because employees operating in Russia or Nigeria are subject to criminal charges for being gay. Even if this is not the case on your team, you may still come up against different systems of belief within your own organization or team related to sexual orientation.

Several years ago in a family-owned business I advised on culturally competent marketing, I overheard a conversation between two colleagues about the founder's son. That conversation went something like this:

Colleague one: "I think he's so funny. I have kind of a work crush on him; my dream is for him to be my gay best friend."

Colleague two: "Totally! He's hilarious. Wait, is he gay?"

Colleague one: "Oh, I'm not being a jerk and saying he's something he's not. His Instagram has pictures with the guy he's seeing on it."

While that may have been true of his Instagram, the founder's son had not shared his sexual orientation with his parents. Since one of his parents *ran the company*, once this person learned people in the office were talking about his sexual orientation, he felt "outed." Even though his colleague was well meaning, her desire to call him her "gay best friend" rather than "best friend" ultimately put him in a situation he did not want to be in with his family and workmates.

Another best practice when talking about sexual orientation is to use identify-first terms like *queer people* or *pansexual people* rather than outdated terms like *homosexuals*. Regardless of the latter term, the person's individual self-identification matters more.

Saying the wrong thing may also be tied to what judgments you make when you think no one will be affected or what you *don't* say that might send an exclusionary message. A long-standing colleague of mine explained that before he was a DEI practitioner, he worked in human resources at a well-known bank. A series of comments and lack thereof pressured him to remove a framed photo of him and his partner on his desk. Namely, he noticed his colleagues would ask about the photos on other people's desks but not his own. His direct supervisor, on the other hand, assumed the person in the photo was a good friend. When my colleague answered that he was his partner, his supervisor laughed it off and said, "Like your business partner? You better not be running a side hustle business on me here!" Finally, my colleague clarified this was his romantic partner, someone he planned to marry, after which his supervisor said nothing and left. The message was clear: his sexual orientation was not something that would be acknowledged here, even though he wanted it to be.

When it comes to sexual orientation, avoiding "outing" your teammates isn't your only responsibility. Understand that language changes quickly and often. Terms we previously thought were positive turn negative, and ones we learned were off limits become the standard.

For example, if we go back to the disability identity, the term *special needs* fell out of favor as members of the disability rights and disability justice communities took control of the language used about them instead of accepting the terms people outside of their communities had originated.

The term *queer* went on the opposite journey. For those who came up in professional environments in the latter half of the twentieth century, a word like *queer* was a slur, plain and simple. Derogatory, demeaning, and offensive, it othered and insulted. As the LGBTQIA2+ movement grew over time and gained more mainstream acceptance, activists decided to take back the word *queer*, changing its connotation from one meant to harm to one meant to include. Now, *queer* is an umbrella term, one that suggests a rejection of traditional binary categories of gender and sexuality.

SOCIOECONOMIC STATUS

Since money is a taboo topic for many workers, it's unlikely that you will have an accurate picture of every colleague's financial situation. As a result, it's important not to casually use stereotyping terms around class, housing, or financial means. Similarly, using deficit-focused language or assuming that financial struggles are a moral or practical *failing* on the part of others promotes harmful messages and divisions among coworkers.

Socioeconomic status is sometimes also referred to as your class and directly relates to your household income. The US reported that, in 2021, the median household income was $79,900 according to the US Census. To qualify as being in the top 1 percent, Knight Frank found you must make $7.9 million per year. For comparison, someone in the 1 percent in India earns $60,000 per year, and someone in the 1 percent in Kenya earns $20,000 a year.

With that said, a poll from Prudential found that 46 percent of Americans consider themselves to be financially struggling, and a survey from Capital One and The Decision Lab reported that 77 percent feel financially anxious.

As part of the management cohort early on in my career at an industrial supplies company, I remember one of my lunchmates pointing out that one of the other cohort participants, who I will call Hayden, was moonlighting as an Uber driver. My lunch group proceeded to speculate about what bad financial decisions this person had made, including spending their paycheck on weekly bottle service. I felt uncomfortable speaking up. I didn't want to be "outed" myself. I had gone without health insurance multiple times throughout my life, experienced a short sale as a result of the 2008 recession, watched my parents spend more than a decade paying off their student loans despite having good jobs, and was secretly working a part-time writing job to pay for housing expenses. I wish I had spoken up, though. I later learned that

Hayden's spouse had accumulated hundreds of thousands of dollars of medical bills in seeking cancer treatment while they were both still in graduate school.

You have a responsibility as a manager to interrupt personal judgments about others around you, even if they do not report to you. Your team members take their cues from you. It's up to you to model inclusive behavior.

TRIBAL OR INDIGENOUS STATUS

Tribal or indigenous status refers to whether you are affiliated with, enrolled in, and belonging to a Native tribe or indigenous group. Many people in this group do not identify as American, which is why the term *Native American* has fallen out of favor in some groups. The term *Indian*, which inaccurately describes indigenous peoples in the language of their colonizers, is also outmoded and potentially offensive. But some indigenous people have reclaimed the terms *American Indian* and *Indian*.

Recently, managers have been asked to adopt land recognition acknowledgments, observe Indigenous Peoples' Day (instead of Columbus Day), or recruit more employees who are enrolled in tribes. Depending on where your company is located geographically, this may be more or less true for you. In my experience working with a variety of companies across the world, many employees have never met someone whom they knew to be indigenous or Native. In the US, especially, this leads to the proliferation of generalizations and stereotypes, often in front of people from these groups who "pass" as White or Latine. All the more reason to use specific references to tribal or indigenous identities and avoid cultural appropriation.

EXCLUSIVE LANGUAGE	INCLUSIVE ALTERNATIVE
low man on the totem pole	junior-level, person of lower rank
powwow	gather or brainstorm
spirit animal	kindred spirit
tribe	community
hold down the fort	take care of
on the warpath	angry, argumentative

POLITICAL AFFILIATION

Political affiliation, sometimes referred to as party affiliation, refers to whether you belong to a certain political party. While many people identify as on the "left" or "right," technically affiliation is related to whether you are registered with a political party. In the US, that may mean being registered with the Republican Party, Democratic Party, Independent Party, Green Party, Libertarian Party, or others. The same parameters around whether a group is dominant or marginalized do not apply because political affiliation is often more of a choice than other identity categories and, because of the nature of the US party system, who holds power changes rapidly and regularly.

Nevertheless, our political affiliations do shape how others view us, especially as political polarization has increased in the last two decades. As Arlie Russell Hochschild notes in *Strangers in Their Own Land: Anger and Mourning on the American Right,* interpolitical marriages are less common than interracial marriages were in 1958. FiveThirtyEight's extensive data analysis on relationships between Republicans and Democrats is summed up in its own report with a telling phrase: "Evidence abounds that Democrats and Republicans really do not like each other."[3]

Talking about politics at work is both increasingly more common and more of a minefield. You may decide your management practice means discouraging or forbidding political discussions. But just because you say not to do something doesn't mean your employees will honor your request. In fact, it may benefit you to take a more flexible position simply so you know what your employees are talking about when you aren't there. Instead, focus on modeling the behaviors you want to see from your employees.

- Don't call people things they don't call themselves or "out" people who wish to keep their political affiliations to themselves.
- Avoid clichés that are party specific. Party registration and political beliefs do not necessarily align, and we tend to either underestimate or overestimate the impact of political affiliation on others' beliefs depending on how we perceive their social identities.
- Don't take for granted that someone would "never say that" or "never interpret it like that." The very concept of common sense is culturally specific and contextual.
- Eliminate words like "right" and "wrong" from your vocabulary, and be open to discussing root issues. Psychologists have shown that people are less distressed by opposing political views than the fact that they disagree with someone they are close to.

INCLUSIVE MANAGEMENT TIP SIX:
AVOID ASSUMPTIONS

Chances are that you have already gone through some form of **unconscious bias** training, which means you know that people associate stereotypes with certain groups that are outside of their immediate conscious awareness. Learning to "check your bias" is really developing the ability to pause before making an assumption about who someone is based on what identities they hold. After all, social identity is how others see you rather than how you see yourself. While you may have experience with people of a certain national origin, socioeconomic status, or education level, it is better to approach every employee with a mindset of curiosity.

PART FOUR

GIVING FEEDBACK AND SETTING GOALS

TRUST—HAVING A CONFIDENT RELATIONSHIP with the unknown—is both necessary and elusive. Giving and receiving feedback feels hard because intentions, motives, and interests are unknowns. This fact becomes even more complicated when issues of identity become part of the conversation, which is why developing nuanced, robust feedback skills that also take into account a diversity of employee goals is so critical to your management practice.

18

WHY IS GIVING
FEEDBACK HARD?

IS THIS FEEDBACK REALLY ABOUT ME or about the stereotypes about people like me? Does this feedback come from a genuine belief in my ability to improve or a desire for me to assimilate to group norms? Would I get this feedback if I held a different set of identities?

These are questions not only your employees will ask but that you will experience too. Part of management is getting used to receiving feedback from all sides: your managers, peers, and employees. Depending on your identities, you may find yourself navigating complex situations in which you both hold power as a manager and are subject to power in your different identity groups.

Take, for example, a manager I work with closely. As a Black woman taking on a new team of direct reports never managed by someone with those intersectional identities, she was acutely aware of her role, position, and presentation. In a sales meeting with a peer, she came very prepared with an introduction that established her credibility as the leader of her department. After the meeting, her direct peer, who was also in attendance, gave her this feedback: "The next time you're in a sales meeting, remember to say that you have a manager and don't *really* run your department. The leadership team does."

This new manager came to me to ask about the feedback. Personally, I was baffled. "But you do run the department. I don't see why saying you have a manager or not matters. Your manager knows you make the final decisions about your department." Interestingly, this peer had not given this feedback to another manager who also stated their role as a department leader but didn't share the same identities.

In other words, bias enters feedback regularly. As a manager, you have to overcome the fear of giving and receiving feedback. You may experience emotional or psychic pain during the experience; you may also cause it. If this makes you wary, remember that growth comes from learning, and well-constructed, thoughtfully delivered feedback is one of our greatest teaching tools in workplaces. The rewards to giving feedback merit the risks, especially when an inclusive, respectful manager makes the practice a regular part of the team environment.

INCLUSIVE MANAGEMENT TIP SEVEN: PRACTICE ENGRAVING

Neuroscience shows us that when we closely watch others do something very well, we start to improve ourselves. For example, the singer Ray LaMontagne developed his distinctive artistic style by very closely and consistently listening to records of blues singers performing at their peak. If you want to develop a healthy feedback culture on your team, adopt this same approach by identifying a few people to watch—either ones you know and can observe in real time or management experts online or at events. Practice adopting their phrases, mannerisms, and attitudes. Then, watch as your own employees do the same by watching you. You don't even have to tell them about engraving or observing how you give feedback; the nature of being a manager is that of receiving constant deliberate attention from the people working for you.

19

WHO GETS FEEDBACK?

NOT EVERYONE RECEIVES FEEDBACK. There's a reason a parable like "The Emperor's New Clothes" exists; out of fear of the consequences, a desire not to engage, or willful, pluralistic ignorance, people may keep the truth about a situation to themselves. The result is that one or more people look foolish, make a terrible mistake, fail to learn or change, or worse.

Of course, there are good, self-protective reasons people don't give feedback to their peers, managers, or employees. What identities a person holds, however, is not one of them. Recent studies from McKinsey about women, Black, and Latine employees in tech demonstrate that these groups receive as much as 20 percent less feedback than men and White employees. In a phenomenon called **protective hesitation**, originated and studied by Harvard professor David A. Thomas, leaders refrain from giving feedback to their employees because of a fear they will seem prejudiced. This fear of seeming sexist, racist, homophobic, transphobic, ableist, or otherwise not only keeps employees unaware of their perceived performance but also helps contribute to their "middling out" or failing to advance in organizations. Making changes in response to critical feedback signals high performance and growth; if that feedback never comes, opportunities become more limited.

It's up to you to make sure you are giving your employees the feedback they need to succeed rather than succumbing to the fear of how they will see you as a result of that feedback. It's also up to you to make sure you are soliciting the feedback you need to improve from all of the people you interact with so that you can continue honing your management skills.

20

GIVING FEEDBACK

SO YOU KNOW YOU NEED TO give your employees feedback, that you hold biases outside of your awareness, and that you may not yet trust yourself in giving unbiased feedback. How can you feel confident in giving constructive feedback? Start by equipping yourself with a few tools that help you develop self-awareness and sensitivity to context around feedback and bias. At first, using the decision tree (see figure 2) may seem overwhelming; after all, there are a lot of steps and questions to ask yourself. The temptation to just not give feedback might be even greater as you go through the process. Resist! Eventually, just like with the inclusive language skills you learned and started integrating in part 3, you will develop muscle memory around checking for bias in giving feedback.

SBIQ[1]

So much of giving high-quality, bias-free feedback is giving feedback on someone's specific behaviors rather than their attributes or characteristics. That is where the **SBIQ (Situation, Behavior, Impact, Question)** framework offers clear guidance. In the model,

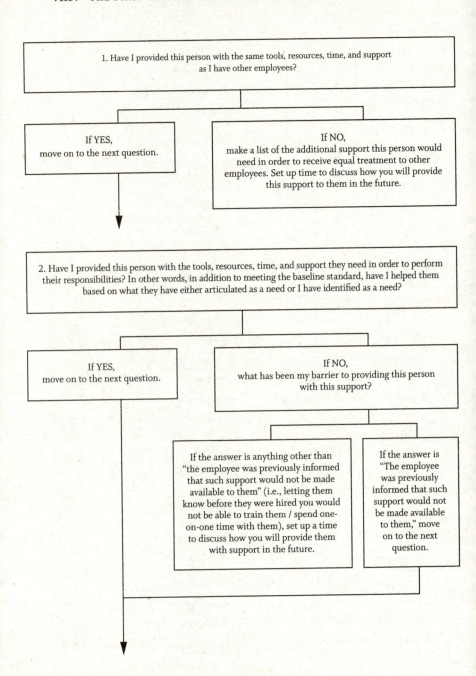

1. Have I provided this person with the same tools, resources, time, and support as I have other employees?

If YES, move on to the next question.

If NO, make a list of the additional support this person would need in order to receive equal treatment to other employees. Set up time to discuss how you will provide this support to them in the future.

2. Have I provided this person with the tools, resources, time, and support they need in order to perform their responsibilities? In other words, in addition to meeting the baseline standard, have I helped them based on what they have either articulated as a need or I have identified as a need?

If YES, move on to the next question.

If NO, what has been my barrier to providing this person with this support?

If the answer is anything other than "the employee was previously informed that such support would not be made available to them" (i.e., letting them know before they were hired you would not be able to train them / spend one-on-one time with them), set up a time to discuss how you will provide them with support in the future.

If the answer is "The employee was previously informed that such support would not be made available to them," move on to the next question.

FIGURE 2

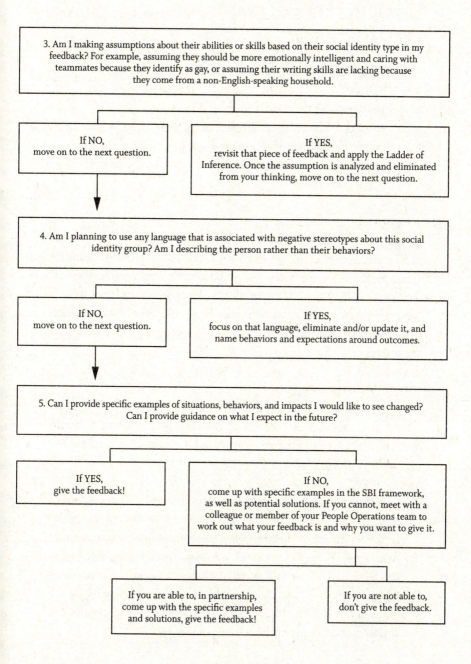

3. Am I making assumptions about their abilities or skills based on their social identity type in my feedback? For example, assuming they should be more emotionally intelligent and caring with teammates because they identify as gay, or assuming their writing skills are lacking because they come from a non-English-speaking household.

If NO,
move on to the next question.

If YES,
revisit that piece of feedback and apply the Ladder of Inference. Once the assumption is analyzed and eliminated from your thinking, move on to the next question.

4. Am I planning to use any language that is associated with negative stereotypes about this social identity group? Am I describing the person rather than their behaviors?

If NO,
move on to the next question.

If YES,
focus on that language, eliminate and/or update it, and name behaviors and expectations around outcomes.

5. Can I provide specific examples of situations, behaviors, and impacts I would like to see changed? Can I provide guidance on what I expect in the future?

If YES,
give the feedback!

If NO,
come up with specific examples in the SBI framework, as well as potential solutions. If you cannot, meet with a colleague or member of your People Operations team to work out what your feedback is and why you want to give it.

If you are able to, in partnership, come up with the specific examples and solutions, give the feedback!

If you are not able to, don't give the feedback.

FIGURE 2

whenever you offer feedback, you must present four key components.

1. **Situation**: What happened? When and where did it happen?
2. **Behavior**: What did the person do?
3. **Impact**: What was the impact of the behavior? Why is giving feedback important as a result?
4. **Question**: What questions do you have for the person about the above?

Throughout your delivery, make sure to keep to the facts and avoid generalizations. Phrases like "you always" or "you never" will most likely cause defensiveness, not to mention undermine your feedback's credibility. In the heat of the discussion, the "Q" component may get lost; be vigilant! The question portion signals you are open to dialogue, curious about the other person's perspective, and willing to collaborate. Let's consider two different examples of SBIQ.

CONSTRUCTIVE FEEDBACK

Imagine that your employee, who happens to be the only man on the team, interrupted several of his colleagues during a brainstorming session about a new product. Using SBIQ, you might say something along the lines of:

In yesterday's team meeting, I noted that a few of your colleagues tried to share ideas about the new product with the group. But before they finished their thoughts, you chimed in with your own. As a result, we were not able to hear from them. I am giving you this feedback because I value your contributions to our brainstorming meetings, and I also want to make sure we create space for others to contribute too. What was your experience of the meeting? And how does it square with what I just shared?

POSITIVE FEEDBACK

On a brighter note, let's imagine another employee in that meeting gave a stellar presentation about the product to start the group discussion off, which was especially impressive considering they had expressed anxiety at having to speak in front of the group. Rather than just offering a basic "good job," you could use SBIQ to reinforce their positive behaviors.

> In yesterday's team meeting, I appreciated how clear, concise, and expert your presentation was—every single person fully understood the feature set. Instead of feeling overwhelmed by the technical details, due to your skillful delivery, everyone felt comfortable brainstorming launch ideas. I know how I felt about your presentation, but how did you feel about it?

NONVIOLENT COMMUNICATION

I credit my teammate Miriame Cherbib with introducing **nonviolent communication** as a standard practice inside of our organization, a valuable feedback tool when situations are especially sensitive. Developed by psychologist Marshall Rosenberg as an alternative to the violent communication he observed as the default in social interactions, nonviolent communication is a language of compassion, one that focuses on achieving what one is seeking in a positive, constructive, and humane way. For this reason, nonviolent communication is an oft-used practice in diversity, equity, and inclusion circles, as well as in education, therapy, diplomacy, and negotiations.

The four components of nonviolent communication are observations, feelings, needs, and requests. Observations rely on stating what you noticed without judgment. After stating an observation, the speaker then articulates how what they noticed made them feel. They connect that feeling to a core need. Importantly, the connection between feelings and needs isn't exclusive to the speaker. In fact, the speaker may consider the same link from their interlocutor's perspective. Finally, the speaker will make a positive, specific, and doable request that focuses on what they *want* rather than what they don't want.

Nonviolent communication–style feedback might take the shape of using four statements that compassionately frame the current situation and present a better future situation and outcome.

- "I noticed . . . [description of a behavior in a specific situation]."
- "This makes me feel . . . [explain how you feel as a result of the situation]."
- "Based on this feeling, I see a connection to . . . [state your need]."
- "Moving forward, I'd like you to . . . [make a request using positive language about the desired behavior]."

If we go back to the constructive feedback first presented using SBIQ, we can note the similarities and differences between approaches. With nonviolent communication, which you might be using with an employee who struggles to receive feedback, your dialogue might take this shape.

- **Observation:** "In yesterday's team meeting, I noticed that when your colleague started sharing a product idea, you volunteered your own before she had finished her thought."
- **Feeling:** "This made me feel anxious about whether we would achieve our goal for the meeting by hearing everyone's ideas."
- **Need:** "I designed these brainstorming sessions because I don't want to move forward with the product until I hear from every team member."
- **Request:** "I'd like you to give Aimee the floor at the start of the next brainstorming meeting."

BALANCING NEEDS

If these approaches to feedback seem like hard work, that's because they are. Sometimes you might feel that giving inclusive, unbiased, compassionate feedback is too much for you to handle on top of everything else you do.

Here's a callback to boundaries; simply put, being an emotionally intelligent manager means knowing when to meet your needs and when to accommodate those of your teammates. Chances are that at some point along your management journey, you will find yourself wondering why your employees cannot just take a piece of factual information, the feedback you offered, and act upon it. As one former coaching client managing a team of six recently put it to me, "Why does telling someone to turn their work in on time have to feel like a therapy session? Just turn your work in on time!"

My reminder to my former client is the same as my reminder to you: you have choices, and you can do anything you want. Just be prepared to deal with the consequences, whatever they may be.

For many new managers, their greatest feedback challenge is engaging with employees who respond to feedback with great sensitivity and emotion. For one, this style is very different from what many of us have been taught about appropriate workplace etiquette, and it's therefore more challenging to respond to at the moment. Second, if you use all of the tools we just learned, you may feel you are already making a tremendous investment of time and energy by giving the feedback. In these situations, consider your needs alongside the needs your employee shares with you in the moment, taking care to balance both instead of automatically placing one above the other.

During a formal performance review with an employee, I used the SBIQ framework to offer constructive feedback. This person expressed shock at the feedback and began to cry. When they recovered themselves, they asked if my feedback meant I thought they were a bad person. I took a breath to center myself and recalibrate to the unexpected response, stated the facts of what I had said, sticking specifically to behaviors I thought could change, and reassured my employee that nothing I had to say had to do with *who* they were but rather how they could improve. My employee began to cry again, so I had a choice to make—do I stay in this meeting until my employee feels better or do I take the five-minute bathroom break I need, prepare for my next meeting, a high-stakes sales presentation, and revisit the situation later? In other words, do I choose my employee's need for validation and resolution, or my basic biological need followed by my desire to perform well in my next meeting? To make the decision, I ran through a quick three-question cycle.

Question: What are our needs?

Answer: My employee has a need for reassurance. I need to take a bathroom break. I also have a need to reset and prepare before delivering a sales pitch.

Question: Which need is more immediate?

Answer: Going to the bathroom is the most immediate need. I also think gathering myself before this sales meeting will benefit the whole team because of the upside revenue potential.

Question: Will there be consequences if I attend to the immediate need over other needs?

Answer: I don't know for sure. Based on past experiences, however, I believe I can set a date and time to resume the conversation with my employee when our emotions settle, and it will be well received.

With this internal calculus, I made the choice to attend to my own needs but invite my direct report to bring this issue back up at another time, by or before our next one-on-one conversation. In that one-on-one, my employee came back with feedback for me, specifically saying that receiving my feedback was painful and they would appreciate it if I delivered it differently. Specifically, they wanted me to frame feedback in the future not as a criticism but as a request. At first, my internal reaction was, "I'm already working so hard and spending so much time on giving you feedback." But I told myself to work through my question cycle again.

Question: What are our needs?

Answer: My employee has a need to receive feedback in a non-threatening way—specifically, that I use nonviolent communication. I have a need to spend less time giving feedback so I can get to other responsibilities. I also have a need to see this employee's performance improve.

Question: Which need is more immediate?

Answer: My employee feels threatened and cannot move on until we find a resolution. I feel overwhelmed by the number of requests coming my way but not at risk or under threat. We both share an immediate need of wanting to move forward.

Question: Will there be consequences if I attend to the immediate need over other needs?

Answer: By adopting the approach my employee recommends, they will feel more supported and motivated to improve. I can *save* time by avoiding future conflicts and honoring my own principle of using nonviolent communication.

Not every compromise will come together as neatly as this one did for me. But more often than not, there is a way to meet both your needs and your employee's, resulting in a win-win.

THE POWER OF PRAISE

People learn so much from their successes and yet spend so little time thinking about them or hearing about them from others. The original authors of *The First-Time Manager* pointed out that using the old adage of "no news is good news" as a management technique leads to lower employee sentiment and higher rates of employee departures.

Still, praise is tricky because people respond to it in such personal ways, especially when they come from historically resilient and nondominant communities. In a brief informal survey of fellow colleagues in the diversity, equity, and inclusion space, practitioners who identified as people with disabilities, members of racially nondominant groups, members of marginalized genders, and people who immigrated to the United States listed out a variety of reasons why praise made them feel comfortable.

> "I'm so used to being told what not to do, what not to be like. I just don't know how to respond when the opposite happens."

> "What do you even say when your boss compliments you? 'Thank you' could backfire because they might think you're full of yourself."

> "I get backhanded compliments so often that I am supposed to be grateful for. Telling me how good my English is . . . that is not a compliment. It's a reminder that you hear my accent and are surprised you can understand me. If anything, now I am more self-conscious."

These data are not meant to discourage you from giving praise. Rather, apply the same thoughtfulness you would to constructive feedback to positive feedback. When offering praise, make sure to:

- ask how they prefer to receive praise—one-on-one, in front of a large group, over email, in person;
- use SBIQ to make sure they know what behavior had a positive impact, along with why it mattered to you or others;
- get their take on how they did; and
- offer encouragement to continue engaging in that behavior or applying that skill in the future.

It's also helpful to keep in mind that negative feedback sticks with people far more than positive feedback. The proportion of praise you offer should take this reality into account. Reinforcing the "good news" in multiple ways over a period of time can help someone view their performance more accurately, since they will be more likely to remember what they need to improve versus what they already hold as a strength and asset.

INCLUSIVE MANAGEMENT TIP EIGHT: ENGAGE IN ROLE-PLAY

As you get used to giving team members feedback, one helpful practice is to role-play the scenario with a trusted peer. Fully commit to talking to that peer as if they are your employee, saying exactly what you plan to say. Take note of where you feel most uncomfortable, if there are different words or phrases you may want to use, and how your peer responds during and after the exchange. Avoid the draw of talking about the feedback you plan to give rather than acting it out; only with direct experience will you be able to tell if you are on the right track!

21

RECEIVING FEEDBACK

NO MATTER HOW ARTFUL AND PRACTICED you are in giving feedback to others, perhaps nothing will have a greater impact on the feedback culture of your team than how you receive constructive feedback. Every single member of your team looks to you to set the tone and model expected behaviors. If you respond to feedback from your employees or your own leaders with openness, thoughtfulness, and accountability, that will start to shape your teammates' reactions to the feedback they receive. The reverse is also true. Being able to identify what kind of feedback might trigger your defensiveness, avoidance, or frustration, as well as preparing a few powerful phrases for responding to people in difficult situations, can help you set an exemplary standard.

UNDERSTANDING YOUR
FEEDBACK TRIGGERS

Who you are as a person will likely inform how you deal with feedback and what kind of feedback you get from others. For example, in the women's leadership group I lead, several of the women I coached noted that they tended to shut down in tough feedback conversations with their employees when their emotionality, specifically whether they came off as "angry Black women," came up. Fear of playing into that stereotype kept them from speaking their minds, asking questions, or even engaging in the conversation at all.

Stereotypes about our identity groups are just one of the many types of triggers that set us off when receiving feedback. If you perceive your character is being called into question, the person delivering feedback is missing important context, or outcomes that are outside of your control are being attributed to you, you may find it hard to stay open and curious. While that's perfectly normal, it's also important to practice self-awareness and manage your emotions to set a positive example and uphold your boundaries. Let me be clear: saying nothing or accepting everything you hear when receiving feedback is *not* a best practice. Listening receptively and offering your experiences, perceptions, and questions is.

To prepare for receiving feedback and ensure you respond intentionally, start by asking yourself: "What really sets me off?" Are you someone who responds well to constructive feedback about a piece of writing but feels totally unprepared for feedback about how you interacted with a colleague? Or do you have a history of receiving, perhaps unfairly, feedback on how you present yourself, which means that a new piece of feedback carries the full weight of the past?

During a particularly tough financial quarter, an employee overseeing a department's budget gave their manager this feedback: "Given where we are relative to our targets, I don't think it was wise for you to approve these expense requests. And it really didn't make sense to invest so much in business development." In the moment, their manager felt the telltale signs of defensiveness—a tightening of the throat muscles, accelerated heart rate, and draining of heat from the face, not to mention some inner dialogue rebuttals forming, like, "And I don't think it's very wise of you to neglect reporting out our financial position on a weekly basis like you promised." But rather than acting on these emotions, this manager took a moment to reflect on a few key questions.

- Am I feeling triggered at this moment?
- What do I think is being said about me?
- How is my body responding at this moment?
- Why might I be reacting in this way?

With these questions in mind, I can start to shift my focus from feeling threatened to assessing the situation and thinking about what it requires. By transitioning from feeling like something is happening to me to remembering my place as a decision-maker in the situation, I reclaim my sense of control and surety.

RESPONDING WITH OPENNESS TO FEEDBACK

Of course, identifying how you are feeling and why is only half of receiving feedback gracefully. The next part is how you show up.

START WITH ACTIVE LISTENING

Active listening is a technique developed in 1957 by Carl Rogers and Richard Farson to facilitate better collaboration in workplaces through a combination of practices, including listening for total meaning by observing verbal and nonverbal cues, recognizing shifts in the speaker's telling, understanding the speaker's perspective, and upholding the integrity of one's own perspective and interpretation.

To engage in active listening, you must first focus your attention and energy on what is taking place. If you find yourself replaying past experiences or thinking ahead to possible solutions, gently nudge yourself back to the present moment. Tune into how the other person appears to you, the environment around you, the words you heard, and how you perceive the tone and tenor behind them.

As you ground yourself in the moment, make sure that you show the person giving you feedback that you are present. This is especially important in situations where you are not in a live, face-to-face setting such as talking over the phone or via video-conferencing. Showing that you are listening might mean nodding, leaning forward, making eye contact, blinking slowly to indicate understanding, or making affirmative sounds.

Further demonstrate you are listening through paraphrasing. Paraphrasing involves synthesizing the content and context of what you have heard, rather than waiting silently or repeating back exactly what you heard. When paraphrasing, make sure you hold on to your own perspective, which includes sticking to "I" statements. Examples of paraphrasing might include: "If I'm understanding you correctly, when I sent that email, it felt undermining to your role as the project manager," or "It sounds like the way I delivered the news was different from what you expected, which was disappointing." In a paraphrase, you are not taking on blame or apologizing; you are getting the facts straight, with an emphasis on capturing what is implicit and explicit.

End a paraphrase with a clarification to ensure mutual understanding and avoid seeming as if you are telling someone else what they think or feel. Questions like "Did I get that right?" and "Are you able to offer more context on what I did in that moment?" can help orient you both.

OFFER A MEASURED RESPONSE

Once you have finished listening to the feedback and fully gathered an understanding of what it means, take a moment to formulate your response. It's important to consider if you *agree or disagree* with the feedback, or if you need more time to think about it. If you agree with the feedback, thank the person for sharing, affirm that you agree, and offer some ideas for how you will incorporate what you learned.

This applies to positive feedback as well as negative feedback. "Thank you for sharing that you liked the way I ran yesterday's meeting. I liked the flow too! I will take your feedback as a signal to update the agenda moving forward." By accepting the praise and incorporating it into a proposed action, you communicate to team members that compliments are valuable sources of information that can lead to helpful team practices.

Now, let's say you disagree with the feedback you received. What do you do, especially if you don't want to seem defensive? Once again, start by thanking the person for sharing—they could have brought this feedback up to someone else or let it sit, leading to anger or resentment in the future, after all. Then try to find some piece of common ground. As factually as possible, state your perspective using "I" statements, any evidence or context that helps illustrate your point, and a proposed resolution. Here's how that manager responded to the feedback on the wisdom of their financial decisions.

> Thank you for sharing your thoughts and raising your concerns. I agree that our financial position is not as strong as we would have hoped, and I know I could have done more to check on our status before approving the expenses. With that said, we have increased the size of our sales pipeline by 40 percent in the last two months as a direct result of those business development investments, which I believe will pay off next quarter. In the future, I think we can work together to keep up real-time cash flow tracking and report our status on a weekly basis, which should help us manage expense requests and determine when and how to make business development investments.

What if you disagree with the feedback and find that you are still triggered? Or that you felt the feedback was offensive or biased? Unfortunately, when you're a manager, this experience is all too common, and you are held to a higher standard of behavior because of the power you hold. That doesn't mean, though, that you must ignore your own boundaries. You can let someone know how you feel or if they made comments you take issue with, so long as you stick to what you know to be true for yourself.

Here are a few examples of respectful disagreements with feedback.

A younger manager to an employee with more years of professional experience:

I find this feedback challenging because, as a younger new manager, I have often heard my experience level cited as a reason for why I should not be in my role. But I am in this role, and I am doing the best I can with the resources available to me.

A manager with caregiving responsibilities to a peer who has none:

I understand that many people believe being a leader means being the last to leave the office and being responsive to email at all hours. That is not my view of leadership or my direct manager's. I try to be fully present in the hours I am at the office and respond to my emails within twenty-four hours; being on-demand at work does not make sense for my family. If you need more from me during the hours I am here, let's talk about what that might look like.

A manager with different socializing preferences than their teammates:

I hear that you'd like more time together. I also think it's important that our social hangouts remain optional rather than mandatory so that we can continue to create space for different needs and preferences on the team. Are there other ways I can show up for you outside of hangouts?

Finally, sometimes you won't know how you feel about the feedback in the situation. In this case, thank the team member for sharing, explain that you need some processing time, and set a specific time when you will get back to them to continue the conversation.

FOLLOW UP ON NEXT ACTIONS

People trust those who follow through on their promises, and the best managers are trustworthy ones. If you promised to change the team agenda, create a more collaborative budgeting system, or offer more transparency into decision-making, you must do so in a timely manner. If you don't think you can commit to a change or improvement, even if you agree with it, then say as much. Do not under any circumstances make a promise you cannot keep. Otherwise, you will compromise your credibility and set an expectation that conflicts on the team are resolved by nodding and smiling, not actually making changes.

In cases where you are unsure, perhaps because the follow-up requires other people whose actions are unpredictable, then name that unknown. You can commit to changes within your control. So, if the feedback you received is about a department-wide change, but you can influence only your direct team, then promise to bring the feedback up to the department lead and report back. Don't promise to roll the change out, even if you're pretty certain you'll be able to get the approval necessary to do it.

ADDRESSING HARASSMENT AND DISCRIMINATION

Being a manager means dealing with situations you never thought would come up before you were a manager.

Here's a true story. A client of mine leading a team of nine direct reports handed me a plain manila folder filled with pages of chat messages between team members on the company messaging platform. One of the team leads had initiated a penis measuring contest where employees measured themselves and posted the results. Needless to say, there had been complaints from some of the team members on the channel, who noted this exchange as an example of **sexual harassment**, one that created a hostile environment. My client asked what he was supposed to do with a situation that felt like it was out of a raunchy teen movie, not a place of business.

Clearly, doing nothing in this situation, or others like it, is not an option. If you work in an organization with a dedicated human resources department, especially one with an employee relationships specialist, take the situation to them immediately. For many small businesses, however, HR is not yet a part of their makeup. If that applies to you and your organization, first investigate if you have an outsourced compliance or HR partner, or even an **Employee Assistance Program** (EAP) from which you might receive resources or counsel. If you don't, escalate the situation to your leadership team. In the event that your leadership team isn't sure what to do, refer to resources and guides from trusted sources to take a collaborative approach with them, such as external corporate counsel or the knowledge library offered through the Society for Human Resource Management (SHRM).

22

MEETING PEOPLE WHERE THEY ARE

HOW MUCH FEEDBACK IS ENOUGH? How much feedback is too much? Unfortunately, there are no specific rules that dictate a perfect feedback ratio or cadence, and as an inclusive manager honoring the individual needs of employees, these questions become even harder to answer. For some employees, informal, real-time feedback coupled with an annual performance review is more than enough to get the information and support they need. For others, quarterly performance reviews paired with weekly checkpoints is the bare minimum.

You have a duty to meet employees where they are, within reason. For those who are less comfortable with feedback, use nonviolent communication before introducing another framework. For those who need more structure, invest time in your formal reviews rather than winging it once you get there. For those who need more informal pulse checks on their performance, set aside time in your regular one-on-one meetings.

But for employees who respond so negatively to feedback they simply won't accept it—that's an issue they will need to work on to develop professionally, not a preference you have to accommodate.

Have an employee who needs complimenting and reassurance *every day*, even when you are slammed with meetings and so much work that you don't even know how they are performing right now? Not only is that outside of the scope of your role, it's probably something you need to give them constructive feedback about. After all, burnout is caused by the demands we place on each other, and while you may hold more power, your employees have the capacity to cause your burnout if they ask more of you than you can give.

In other words, developing team-wide sustainable feedback practices involves delicately balancing group needs with individual interests. Yours included.

DEVELOPING SUSTAINABLE FEEDBACK PRACTICES

The basic challenge of creating a feedback culture is ensuring feedback continues as you add more and more people. There will be times in your management career when this feels beside the point, namely because you have enough time to do all of your work and manage your team members. But if you're like most of the managers I know, this situation is the exception to the rule.

To create sustainable feedback practices, keep these principles in mind.

1. **Formalize the structures; personalize the delivery.** If you're going to keep up with feedback, set up a clear timeline, format, cadence, and communication framework. If you are going to give feedback weekly, make sure it's part of some structure—a department check-in, a one-on-one meeting, or online communication via an employee engagement platform. Once you have the scaffolding, you can fill it with what each person needs.

One teammate may need lots of reassurance and validation in that one-on-one, while another just wants a clear target for next week. The dedicated time for feedback that *everyone* has available can be customized for them.

2. **Less but better.** Don't make the mistake of thinking more is better. Not all feedback is helpful, as we've learned, and sometimes we just don't have anything to say. Make a point of always delivering thorough, robust feedback rather than trying to generate more of it.

3. **Decisively commit, adaptively evolve.** If as a team you decide you need to do in-person, all-team project retrospectives every six weeks, then do project retrospectives every six weeks. Calendar them out, set up the agendas, and make sure people have time to prepare for them. But if after the first few, you realize that they need to happen via shared comments instead of in physical meetings and only among project leads, adapt! Don't waste time by waiting to try a feedback practice everyone supports; do transform the practice once you have more experience with how well it works.

INCLUSIVE MANAGEMENT TIP NINE: TRY AN AFTER ACTION REVIEW

To get your team into the habit of giving and receiving feedback across all levels and about different types of work, introduce an After Action Review, which is sometimes called a postmortem. This is a review where team members evaluate a project to develop insights that inform future projects by reflecting on its successes and areas for improvement. For major initiatives, adopting a regular After Action Review process strengthens a team's feedback culture while contributing to better project outcomes in the future. For an especially productive After Action Review meeting, complete a premeeting form to record individual feedback, host a moderated meeting with a designated facilitator, capture key, agreed-upon insights in easy-to-access space, and send a follow-up detailing how these insights are being used two to six weeks later.

Access an After Action Review template at
alidamirandawolff.com/bookreaders.

PART FIVE

MANAGING CONFLICT

CONFLICT ISN'T INHERENTLY BAD OR UNHEALTHY. Conflicts arise when two or more ideas clash. This clashing can be generative, like how tectonic plates clashing sometimes result in new landmasses or mountain ranges. Inclusive managers often encounter more explicit conflict because they create the space for more ideas to come into contact and more types of people to engage in their development. In fact, this is part of why diverse teams have been shown to be more profitable and successful—the coming together of many different perspectives and ways of working has greater potential to breed new and inventive outputs.

REBRANDING CONFLICT

But conflict is uncomfortable and destabilizing. For many people, it tops the list of their greatest fears, in part because the promise of reconciliation, resolution, or repair seems uncertain. Not only that, but the wrong kinds of conflict can wreck a team. It's hard to imagine a successful soccer team made up of players fighting one another on the field during the game. Too often, managers see their roles when it comes to conflict as serving as the referees— making a call in one person's favor and demeriting another, pulling people out of the game, and policing the game rather than playing in it.

I think it's time for a rebrand. Managers should act as team captains, bringing their players together before red cards ever show up. By working beside their teammates and collaborating to enact a good working life for everyone, they can see all of the benefits of creative conflict without fearing its more destructive potential outcomes.

INCLUSIVE MANAGEMENT TIP TEN:
PRACTICE HEALTHY, STRUCTURED CONFLICT

Remove the stigma from conflict by creating spaces for healthy conflict, like **fishbowl conversations**. Present an idea, and ask team members to discuss and debate its merits. You might even consider assigning positions on the idea at random, asking those in support of an idea to argue against it and vice versa.

23

MANAGING YOUR EMOTIONS

EVEN WITH MANAGEMENT TRAINING, TOOLS, AND FRAMEWORKS at your disposal, managing conflict is easier in theory than in practice, in part because you are a human being with emotions, not some manager-AI capable of perfectly executing the same script over and over again.

In order to navigate conflict on your team, especially in the wake of society-wide issues like identity-based violence, public health crises, and natural disasters that disproportionately impact marginalized groups, you must have a strong sense of emotional self-awareness and the ability to manage your emotions in real time.

Imagine a bucket filled with water. You place a bright red balloon in the bucket and submerge it. You find that as long as you keep pushing the balloon down to the bottom of the bucket with your hand, it stays there. The second you lessen the pressure on the balloon or let go altogether, however, the balloon pops right back up to the surface. You try pushing it down again, splashing water out of the bucket, but once again, when you let go, the balloon pops right back up.

This red balloon is a negative emotion. During conflict-laden conversations about our social identities, we often find ourselves overtaken by emotional bad weather. Many of us are taught not to express negativity at work as individual contributors, and when we become managers, we are warned by mentors and business books alike against seeming "too emotional" with our colleagues and customers. This is especially true of folks from nondominant groups, such as folks from marginalized genders, races, and ages. When faced with our own metaphorical balloon in a bucket, we feel the urge to push it down. The problem is that when our attention shifts or something else requires our focus or composure, that emotion pops up. The more we push it down, the harder the emotion is to control, resulting in an inappropriate outburst, an unkind comment, an unwanted burst of tears, or something else.

If we want to direct and guide our emotions, we have to address them at the surface, not continuously submerge them. When a challenging emotion arises during a conflict, try to visualize it. Ask yourself, "Where am I noticing this emotion in my body? What emotion is it? Why am I experiencing it?" You may even choose to name that emotion in the conversation itself by saying something like, "When I hear you say this, I feel frustrated," or "I am trying to listen, and I also need a moment to process some of my own anxiety in order to be fully present with you." It can be helpful to have some go-to phrases to turn to when conflicts arise. A few that strike the balance of honoring your own humanity while maintaining composure for those looking to you as their leader are:

- "I need a moment to process that. Might we pause for a few moments?"
- "Thank you for sharing. This information is new to me. I may need some time for it to sink in."
- "I would like to collect myself. Can we come back to this topic later today?"

As the conflict progresses, don't forget to monitor your own emotional state. Check in with yourself to ask: "Where is my balloon? What am I pushing down that I need to address, either internally or in this conversation, in order to guide how I feel?"

24

DEALING WITH
UNWANTED EMOTIONS

IN 2020, MY HUSBAND AND I PURCHASED our first home and immediately set ourselves to ripping out the lawn and planting a pollinator garden made up of only native plants. This was a dream of ours, especially in a place like Illinois where so much of the native prairie has been razed, endangering habitats for a variety of insects and animals that live only in this region. While native plant gardens are a lot less maintenance than traditional yards, they face many threats. One of those threats is wild garlic mustard, which flies under the radar before decimating populations of native plants.

I have come to associate uninvited, unwanted emotions with wild garlic mustard. Some emotions we choose to hold on to and welcome into our emotional gardens; others we don't, but they still take root. When we enter conversations about identity, we have plenty of feelings about our own identities and those of others, some of which we embrace and others we might not even know are there. When we chance upon the invasive plants, our first inclination is to whack some weeds. We don't want them messing up our gardens, so we try to destroy them quickly. When we face a weed like wild garlic mustard, which has a slender white taproot that buds, establishing a widespread colony before we even notice, that strategy simply does not work. As long as that taproot is in the ground growing buds, we can whack and whack, but it will live on and spread.

The same is true of your emotional ecosystem. When confronted with conversations that uncover or unleash difficult emotions, our quick impulse to cut them out *right now* doesn't address the heart of the matter. Our anger, sadness, frustration, and fear—the emotions we didn't choose and were likely put there by other people, experiences, or messages—all have their own taproots. In order to remove them from our gardens, we have to find their centers and pull them up by their roots. Otherwise, they will keep reproducing themselves.

25

NAVIGATING CONFLICT WITH COMPASSIONATE CONVERSATIONS

HAVE YOU EVER BEEN PART OF a conversation that went so wrong, you questioned your career, your life purpose, and even your own values? I have.

In fact, I have so many times that finally I decided to develop my own method for engaging in conflict. It was only after I developed and started using the framework that fellow managers and peers asked me how I was coming out of such tough situations—disagreements between team members about discrimination, volatile exchanges that played into negative stereotypes, or insensitive or invalidating arguments where folks said things they regretted long afterward—with stronger relationships and a deeper collective understanding of the team. Since they seemed keen to try out the method, I gave it a name: Compassionate Conversations.

The Compassionate Conversations framework (see figure 3) is a simple five-part method designed to leverage both the psychological and social benefits of compassionate empathy and being in service of others. Put simply, it's a cheat sheet for how to regulate yourself emotionally while also being able to talk to others, especially those you don't agree with, in a way that is caring, open, and dedicated to achieving mutually beneficial outcomes.

The Compassionate Conversations Framework

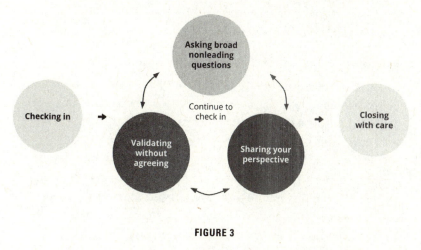

FIGURE 3

STEP ONE:
CHECKING IN

Every Compassionate Conversation begins with checking in. Checking in refers to asking the person or people you want to talk to how they are feeling and determining whether now is the appropriate time to initiate a deeper dialogue. If one of you is too distracted, emotionally hijacked, unwilling to engage in a process, or averse to sharing their feelings and reactions, a Compassionate Conversation will not be possible.

If you decide you are all in the right psychological frame of mind to engage, you will use the information you gleaned to structure your approach. Importantly, while you begin with a check-in, the process of checking in doesn't end once you initiate the conversation. You will continue checking in as the conversation progresses, giving space for anyone involved to pause or regroup along the way.

STEP TWO:
ASKING BROAD, NONLEADING QUESTIONS

Introduce exploratory questions that don't presume an answer or orientation. These are questions that are open-ended and allow for others to help steer the conversation too. These questions are asked for the purpose of better understanding another person, not collecting information to help you "win" the conversation.

How do you know if a question is broad enough and doesn't presume an answer? First, check to make sure it passes the open-ended test. Are there more than two answers a person could logically provide to the question? Is there room for you to be surprised by what they say? Is the question a probe seeking meaning? Could you have your mind changed by the answer?

That last point is especially important. If you are framing your questions with clauses like "Wouldn't you agree," "Don't you think," or "Shouldn't you," you are presuming an answer and guiding them toward it. Better questions tend to start with "how" and "what."

STEP THREE:
VALIDATE WITHOUT AGREEING

In leading healing sessions over the last decade, the most important lesson I've learned is this: folks don't need you to understand; they need you to *believe them*. To validate someone does not mean forfeiting your own perspective or asserting you know more than you do. The truth is that you may never understand someone else's feelings or experiences; and you can still accept something is true for someone else, even if it is not true for you.

For example, a queer employee might say that because they are a gay man, they are often pigeonholed by colleagues into doing stereotypically "feminine" tasks that don't interest them. You may be a straight person, a gay person who hasn't felt this way before, or simply so new to the situation that you don't have context. That's okay—you don't have to say, "I agree," or "That's true." You can, though, acknowledge that you hear them and you believe in the distress they feel.

Validating statements to add to your toolbox for high-conflict situations include:

- I hear you.
- I believe you.
- I can see how this might impact you.
- I can understand how this affects you.
- Here's what I am gathering (with a statement of what you heard).
- It sounds like (with a statement of what you heard).
- Thank you for being willing to tell me.
- It makes sense you would (feel/react/respond) that way.
- That must have been (difficult/frustrating/hard/gratifying/important) for you.

STEP FOUR:
SHARING YOUR PERSPECTIVE

After saying something like, "I can see how this might impact you," you absolutely have a right (and in this framework, a mandate) to follow up with, "This is how it affected me," or "Let's hear how it affected this other person in the conversation."

The key in sharing your perspective is to speak for yourself and only for yourself. That means using "I" statements and refraining from bringing other people's opinions, views, or feelings into the conversation if they are not there to share them. Since the goal of a Compassionate Conversation is a constructive and caring solution, this step is also an opportunity to acknowledge points of mutuality or connection from the other person's perspective when expressing your own.

STEP FIVE:
CLOSING WITH CARE

Compassionate Conversations are intense and sometimes tiring. You wouldn't be alone in wanting to end the conversation once you think you've completed step four. Yet this strategy opens up several possible issues in the future. You might think you both agreed to the solution when you didn't or that you understood each other when a vital piece of communication is missing. You might also leave lacking a sense of closure, making future encounters awkward or unpleasant. A fear of awkwardness might lead to avoiding one another, which keeps a conflict open even longer.

Closing with care involves offering gratitude for the other's participation in the conversation, aligning on clearly defined next steps, checking out by sharing the state you are leaving the conversation in, and, if applicable, setting a time to reconnect in the near future.

Here's an example of what you might say when you close with care.

I really appreciate you taking the time to unpack this issue with me. I am grateful for your honesty and willingness to share. Based on this conversation, we will clear up the misunderstanding with the rest of the team during our next department meeting. We will meet ahead of time to align on who will say what. Personally, I am leaving this conversation feeling hopeful, if a little wiped out. If it's okay with you, can we touch base tomorrow morning to see how we're both feeling after we've had time to process this conversation?

26

DIFFERENT TYPES
OF CONFLICT

MANAGER-EMPLOYEE CONFLICTS

Throughout your management journey, you will face many different types of conflict. The first type to prepare yourself for is between your employee and you. Whether you hurt each other's feelings, disagree about performance, or have to part ways about how creative and generative the experience is (as opposed to how adversarial and destructive) depends on the two of you.

WHEN IT'S YOUR IDENTITY AT STAKE

Recently, I was in a team-building session with several other people. We invented mythical characters for ourselves with the intention of talking about our identities inside and outside of work in new ways. Since the goal was to learn more about one another's identities, I chose to create a character with a mobility disability similar to mine. I saw this as an act of reclamation and an opportunity to celebrate my disability. Another game player built on my description by framing my character's disability as a fatal flaw and "gifted" me a magical cane. I suddenly noticed a soreness spreading across my chest. "Oh no," I thought, "am I hurt?"

As the example demonstrates, you might already be on the receiving end of a microaggression or a series of microaggressions. And manager or not, you deserve an opportunity for repair if that's what you need. Here's how you can engage in this repair using the Compassionate Conversations model.

Checking in: Check in with yourself and ask what you need in order to heal. Then, go to whomever you want the apology from and gauge whether they can provide it. Do not feel pressured to make yourself feel unsafe; this is about what you need.

Asking broad, nonleading questions: Only follow this step if you want to understand why they did what they did. It's useful for context gathering; not so much if what you need is a straightforward, "I'm sorry."

Validating without agreeing: You may meet resistance from a defensive interlocutor. Destabilize the resistance by saying, "I hear you," or "I believe that was your intention." Avoid statements like, "That makes sense," or "I get it," which might indicate to them that their behavior was acceptable to you. Of course, if they cleared something up and it now is acceptable to you, then feel free.

Sharing your perspective: Share only as much as feels comfortable to you. Being vulnerable opens you up to more potential harm, so take only as much risk as you feel is right for you. If you can be open and vulnerable, focus on "I" statements and what a better way forward would be.

Closing with care: Set next steps or expectations for the future. If at any point the conversation takes a turn for the worse, know that you have the right to take some moments away and breathe. If the conversation becomes very fraught, give yourself the space to decide whether you want to revisit it or if you want to end the dialogue altogether.

PERFORMANCE IMPROVEMENT

Many philosophies on performance improvement exist. Some organizations ascribe to the idea of "hire slowly, fire quickly," while others embrace the power of a Performance Improvement Plan as a vehicle for transformational change. You will likely develop your own perspective as you mature in your management practice. You will also have to adopt your organization's policies and approaches. In other words, if there's a difference in your perspective and the organization's, your relationship to performance is already one of conflict. And that's without even accounting for the employee, who will bring their own views and emotions to the situation.

In other words, performance improvement is the quintessential conflict type managers confront. Applying the Compassionate Conversations framework to this type of conflict may feel especially difficult—if HR is fundamentally wrong, or your employee is demonstrably and perhaps unashamedly underperforming, how are you supposed to follow these steps?

Checking in: Take yourself through the performance feedback bias decision tree (chapter 20) before having the performance conversation with your employee to make sure you are coming from an inclusive, equitable position. At the start of the conversation, affirm this is a feedback conversation and ask your interlocutor how they are entering the space. Regardless of how they enter, you can proceed with the conversation—you're just taking their mindset into consideration.

Asking broad, nonleading questions: Without fail, always, always, always start a performance feedback conversation by asking the other person how they think they are performing or performed in a specific instance. Only share your feedback after you've heard their self-evaluation. You must understand if there is a disconnect in order to proceed.

Validating without agreeing: Affirm lived experiences, repeat back any information you don't quite understand for clarification, and create space for them to add anything they think they have missed.

Sharing your perspective: Provide your feedback by naming specific situations, what the person did or did not do, and the impact of their actions. Keep your focus narrow and your description detailed. Do not make any value judgments or use the language of extremes, such as "You always do this," or "I think you're just a disorganized person."

Closing with care: Name exactly what you expect the person to do leaving the conversation, as well as one to three actions you will take to help them implement the feedback. If you expect the employee to study a **Performance Improvement Plan**, assign a due date. Access a Performance Improvement Plan template at **alidamirandawolff.com/bookreaders**.

TERMINATIONS

There is such a thing as giving an employee a graceful exit, as implausible as that may seem to anyone who has terminated an employee. By sticking to the Compassionate Conversations framework, and yes, balancing individual interests and group needs, you can navigate what will likely be one of the hardest and most uncomfortable experiences you will have as a manager.

Take this real-life management example. After painstaking back-and-forth conversations and two negative performance reviews, I knew it was time to let my employee, who I will call Blaise, go. They were unhappy, and everyone else on the team noticed. Their writing skills failed to meet our organizational needs, more than 80 percent of the job was writing, and . . . they hated writing. No one likes to feel like they're doing a bad job or to feel stuck doing work they don't like. Yet they didn't want to leave of their own accord. By their own admission, there were a few reasons they didn't want to quit. Blaise liked the culture and their teammates; they appreciated being able to set their own schedule; and, most importantly, they were a single parent with two kids. They were afraid of losing health insurance and a stable source of income. Before writing a separation agreement or scheduling a termination meeting, I initiated a Compassionate Conversation with Blaise. Here's how I used the steps.

Checking in: I stated what kind of conversation I intended to have and why. I checked to make sure this wasn't a surprise and that Blaise was prepared to engage.

Asking broad, nonleading questions: I asked if Blaise would be open to a thought experiment. I also presented two core questions.

- What do you want for yourself at work?
- What do you think the team needs from this role?

Validating without agreeing: I did not debate what Blaise wanted for themselves. I also acknowledged how difficult it was to rely on a job to be able to meet basic human needs, like health care and the money to pay rent and buy food. I thanked Blaise for being so honest.

Sharing your perspective: I left room to respond to Blaise's statements with potential solutions, such as a longer transition time to give them the space to find a new role and reduce any gaps between paychecks. The caveat would be that the role would be more administrative and focus on the tasks that no one was getting to but needed to take place to keep the operations running smoothly. I also reiterated that our policy is to pay for three months of health insurance after an employee is terminated and then offer twenty-four months of COBRA.

Closing with care: We both stated what we believed we were taking away from the conversation and aligned on our next steps, which was a thirty-day transition period with the option for administrative hourly contract work on the table if Blaise had not already secured a new position and a guaranteed three months of covered health insurance followed by an option to stay on our plan via COBRA.

WHAT ABOUT LAYOFFS?[1]

While you may be responsible for the individual culture of your team, the combination of market conditions and the overall financial health of your organization is not up to you. I won't sugarcoat it: most layoffs create a ripple effect of financial insecurity, psychological distress, and grief. The research shows that it takes two years to recover from the trauma of job loss.[2] If you have already decided that a layoff is inevitable, then your responsibility as a leader is to reduce the amount of harm that decision will create.

Part of that, naturally, is using the Compassionate Conversations framework to give people a space to express themselves, resonate with them, and offer your words of encouragement or care. After all, inviting hundreds of employees who are performing well and serving the organization loyally to a previously unplanned videoconference and announcing they are being let go and will lose access to their accounts and devices is not exactly inclusive, compassionate, or good leadership.

Checking in: A check-in during a layoff is more delicate because so much is outside of your control. Simply offer that you are willing to listen to comments or questions your employees have.

Asking broad, nonleading questions: "Broad" and "nonleading" take on a different character during a layoff conversation. Ask if they understand what is taking place and if they are aware of the resources available to them.

Validating without agreeing: This is where the art of holding space, or accepting and supporting others without judgment while still recognizing your own boundaries, becomes most important. Express empathy, acknowledge the difficulty of the situation, and whatever you do, don't argue or contradict as your employee shares their experiences. Remember, this is an emotional time, and they may say things they wouldn't otherwise.

Sharing your perspective: Express your sadness at having to deliver this news. Wish your employee well. If appropriate to your relationship, offer recommendations, tools, or resources that might help them find another opportunity.

Closing with care: Sum up the key information from the conversation and extend an invitation to continue your relationship as professional peers outside of the organization.

As might seem obvious by now, a Compassionate Conversation fails to satisfyingly address this type of conflict—it's a breakup where the two of you don't want to break up, a manufactured conflict in which you are unfortunately on different sides, with you having to make the break and the employee wishing that weren't the case. That's why creating a more personal, caring exit process is worthwhile in a worst-case scenario that will have lasting impacts on those affected. To develop this process, first consider measuring layoff outcomes not by how quickly or cheaply you can lead the process but, instead, by being able to address these questions either on your own or in conjunction with your HR team.

- Have you created a clear communication plan with multiple stages that allow employees to plan their next steps?
- Does every employee affected understand their severance package? Do they have someone they can directly speak with to understand its details?

- Does every employee understand COBRA or other programs related to their benefits upon their exit? If they will be eligible for unemployment, do you have easy-to-understand instructions to share? Will they have access to outside resources you can provide should they need help claiming benefits in the future?
- Have you directed employees who won't be affected by layoff to help their colleagues who will?
- Are you measuring the process's effectiveness by how many employees you connect with opportunities?
- Will employees be "locked out" of their accounts immediately upon notice? Or is there a space or place where they can say goodbye?
- If they will lose access to their accounts, can they opt in to sharing their contact information with colleagues in one centralized place?
- Are some of the folks affected in the same geographic area? Do they know they are? Is there a way to communicate meetup details or gather information they can access post-layoff?

Another important guiding question for leading layoffs with compassion and humanity is: "Who will this decision serve?"

If a layoff really is the only option, this question can help uphold the importance of your employees over competing interests. For example, while it may not serve shareholders or fellow managers afraid to lose high-performing employees to offer advance notice, such notice *will* serve employees who need to plan for an uncertain future. During Nokia's restructure in 2011, the organization gave employees a one-year notice, with managers and HR professionals focusing on helping them secure other opportunities either internally or externally.

Similarly, at one of our client organizations, the People team let members of their team know that layoffs were planned but who would be directly affected by them was still unknown. While this sense of uncertainty may have been discombobulating in the short term, ultimately, when the news came, employees were more mentally and financially prepared. Offering advance notice also forces you to consider what you can do for employees before their official final days. Whether it's investing in education or training programs, compiling a list of affected employees to circulate across your networks, or pressuring your leadership to make sure leave and paid time off commitments are met, these earlier interventions could make a significant difference to employees.

TEAM CONFLICTS

Even when you aren't in direct conflict with your team members, you may still find yourself embroiled in conflict. The more inclusive, compassionate, and trustworthy you are, the more you will hear about problems, frustrations, and disagreements. Take the tide of "bad news" as a sign that you are doing your job well. Then, set up practices that prioritize fair outcomes for everyone, yourself included.

BETWEEN YOUR TEAM MEMBERS

As a manager, you will often be asked to resolve issues between your immediate direct reports. Preparing yourself for these situations and cultivating even, balanced relationships with employees will help keep these conflicts in the healthy zone.

Take this example from a new manager at a software-as-a-service company. The product team launched an updated version of its web-based customer chat feature. Within a few days of the rollout, a major conflict erupted in the worst possible way—over chat messages in the company's public messaging channel. One employee had changed some of the help text in the chat system without discussing it with the colleague in charge of the feature update. Their colleague had called them out for breaking the process and "disrespecting the team" by going rogue. Within a few hours, three other employees had weighed in, taking sides in the process.

By first collecting information through broad, nonleading questions after determining both parties were receptive, the manager was able to home in on the core issues, create an atmosphere of nonjudgment, and share a perspective that helped the employees reach a resolution. Here is how you could do the same.

Checking in: Start by making sure that your teammates are *ready* to have the conversation with each other. Ask how they are doing, what is going on, and if anything is coming up for them that may keep them from being present. If you determine they are in a calm and neutral space, set up a three-way conversation. If not, reschedule, but be sure to let them know you *will* be having this conversation according to a clearly defined timetable.

Asking broad, nonleading questions: Always start with the biggest, most open-ended question, working your way down to more specific questions. Use your questions to help them come to their own insights as you discuss. You might try the following sequence.

- What is your perspective on the product feature launch? In your own words, are you able to describe your understanding of how this launch was supposed to happen?
- What, if anything, would you like to better understand about why the launch was structured the way it was?
- What, if anything, would you like to better understand about your colleague's actions or reactions?
- What, if anything, would you like to better understand about your colleague's role on the team more generally?

Validating without agreeing: Repeat back what you've heard and use validating but neutral statements. Note that you *will* be agreeing with some of what each person says because you cannot challenge their lived experiences, but you will never say "I agree" or "I'm totally with you" to anything they share. Below are some example responses.

Example One

Project leader: "You can't just change the rules because you want to! It's not how we work here!"

You: "What resonates with me is that you feel that the rules are changing really fast, and they don't align with what you have experienced here before."

Example Two

Project supporter: "Using these arbitrary workflow guidelines doesn't square with our commitment to put customers first. That help text was a direct response to customer feedback."

You: "I hear you when you say that you believe these guidelines don't align with your understanding of our team values, which makes using them difficult."

Sharing your perspective: It's at this point when you've provided some validation that you will share your perspective. You will answer any open questions your employees present about their roles and your expectations. If you believe you may have contributed to the conflict, you may name it here. Otherwise, state exactly how you want the team to run in the future.

Closing with care: Sum up the conversation as factually as possible, allow for the teammates to present follow-up questions or concerns, and then agree to next steps. In a case like this one, agree to *actions*, such as having them repeat back their roles, work on another project together as a "redo" attempt at collaboration, and apologize to their teammates for bringing the conflict to the team level.

BETWEEN YOUR TEAM MEMBERS AND LEADERS

Your employees exist in the broader organizational ecosystem, not just on your immediate team. That means you may find yourself mediating conflicts between your direct reports and your leaders, a surreal experience that few management resources address. With millennials and Gen Z employees, in particular, self-expression and authenticity rank significantly higher in their order of needs than with other generations. Given this phenomenon, the likelihood that your employees and leaders may come into conflict is even greater.

At one of our client organizations, this sort of conflict erupted over a comment in an all-company meeting. The director of marketing reported the company's efforts around community outreach and commitments to antiracism. During the question-and-answer portion of the meeting, a new manager's employee publicly expressed reservations about these efforts. "I don't think we can ever be an antiracist organization with our current CEO in charge. He's the opposite of an antiracist."

Predictably, the CEO was hurt, offended, and angry. The director of marketing had ended the meeting, but the damage was done. The CEO immediately called the new manager. "This is exactly why I didn't want to do this antiracism stuff. Are we sure this was even about antiracism? Or would you say your employee is disgruntled? Underperforming? We cannot have this kind of mudslinging!"

In a thoughtful, measured, and highly empathetic use of the Compassionate Conversations framework, the manager was able to dig into why the CEO felt so hurt and what he was afraid of when it came to antiracism work. By relying heavily on nonviolent communication practices, the manager was able to help the CEO to separate himself as a person from the role and institution he represented to consider employee doubts about antiracism in his organization. The result was an emotional hour of admissions, which ultimately led to him taking accountability for nonparticipation in the organization's stated commitment to support Black employees, customers, and community members.

If you find yourself in this situation, determine how far you are willing to go in the conversation. Responding to someone who holds racist, ableist, sexist, antireligious, transphobic, or elitist beliefs, to name a few, is hard-core emotional work that often feels very unsafe. If you feel directly threatened, it is always okay to opt out and instead seek out an ally or advocate to engage in the conversation instead. You always have the right to say no to someone who wants to debate these issues with you at work. And that no does not have to come with an explanation. Here's how you might use the framework if you do decide to engage.

WITH YOUR LEADER

Checking in: Start with a more general check-in on how they are doing and feeling. Spend the first few minutes setting mutually agreed-upon ground rules for an empathetic discussion. A few I like are listed.

- Address behaviors over individual characteristics or traits.
- Avoid phrases like "you should" and "why didn't you?"
- Use phrases like "I hear you" and "I believe you."
- Don't expect to solve everything in this conversation; instead, focus on feeling connected.

Asking broad, nonleading questions: The power dynamics in a situation like this are complicated, especially when you are caught in the middle of people with very different relationships to power. Understand that extra tenderness may be required in how you ask questions.

Validating without agreeing: Remember, you do not have to tolerate offensive language or continue a hostile conversation, just as you do not have to make someone feel "good" about the things they have said because they are your boss or boss's boss. If you wish to continue the conversation, invoke your ground rules as much as possible.

Sharing your perspective: An empathetic approach is one that draws on an understanding of the other person's lived experience and closely held beliefs, as well as your own. Emphasize your appreciation for their openness, vulnerability, and authenticity, and explain that you will offer your own.

Closing with care: Leave time for a checkout. Do you understand the next steps? Will you involve your employee in a three-way conversation? Is the matter resolved?

WITH YOUR EMPLOYEE

In this kind of conversation, it often makes sense to talk to both parties separately before ever bringing them together. With this example, since the CEO directly called the manager, it was clear who the manager would talk to first. But what about the employee, who potentially just put their job, or at least their reputation, at risk by making a statement against the CEO publicly? You might initiate a Compassionate Conversation with the employee like this.

Checking in: Consider their role, how close they are to the issue, what identities they hold, and what kind of relationship you have with them. Based on your assessment, tailor how you balance cooperativeness versus assertiveness in conducting your check-in. You may decide the employee was right to say what they did when they said it; you might not. The point is you need to know before you initiate a dialogue with them.

Asking broad, nonleading questions: All of the same rules apply during this part of the conversation as with the leader. Since you'll likely be doing some vulnerable sharing, make sure your questions invite the same level of openness but don't *require* them. Remember, vulnerability is a privilege not everyone can afford, and your direct report may not feel it's one they hold with you. In fact, you may be feeling this yourself as you enter the conversation. If you were addressing this particular situation, you might ask the following questions:

- What does the term "antiracism" mean to you? What is it associated with?
- Are there principles, ideas, or personal associations of antiracism that specifically speak to you?
- Why does our organization being antiracist matter to you? What, if anything, would it change or improve for you?
- What do you see as our leadership team's roles in antiracism? Our CEO's?

Validating without agreeing: Avoid the temptation to flip their responses to the questions above into one that leads to compromise or resolution with leaders right away. For example, if they say, "I want the organization to be antiracist because I want it to honor and respect everyone who works here," don't respond with, "That's true for our CEO too!" This is a space to affirm what you have heard them say, not convince them of another position.

Sharing your perspective: Mentally recap the ground rules, and share what you have heard, how you understand it, and what you want the other person to understand. Leave the conversation open to evolution. In other words, listen closely enough to be changed by what you hear *and* give them the opportunity for the same. We want to achieve common ground with a Compassionate Conversation, not "win."

Closing with care: Provide a clear blueprint of what you think will happen next, not only with you but with the leader too. Do not make promises you cannot keep; only commit to what is in your control.

IDENTITY-BASED CONFLICTS

BETWEEN COWORKERS

It's amazing what comes up inside of organizations when you bring together a diverse group of people. In an all-team training session with a large nonprofit organization, I asked the participants to reflect on a time when they thought about their race at work and then break out into small groups to discuss what came up. When we reconvened, I asked for volunteers to share some of the key insights that arose from their discussions. What followed landed as a shock with almost everyone on the team. An employee shared, "In our group, I met Jay for the first time. He's on the maintenance team, and I'm in the field, so we never crossed paths. He said he thought about his race every time his coworkers casually used the N-word. Never in a million years did I think that kind of language would be used here. But it is." The room broke out into frenzied chatter until Jay's manager raised her hand. "Jay, I had no idea this was happening. Why didn't you ever tell us about it?" Jay's response was concise. "No one ever asked," he said.

Instead of shutting down the conversation or moving on to other exercises for the sake of time, my cofacilitator and I chose to stay with the issue—with Jay's permission, of course—and work through the Compassionate Conversation framework as an organization. The result was a tense, awkward, and ultimately healing conversation about the power of language, whose voices are listened to, and what to do when there is a fundamental breakdown in company mores.

What important issues have gone unaddressed in your organization simply because no one ever asked? How might you be the one to ask? Let's break down what worked in the training session after Jay shared and think through how a Compassionate Conversation might help answer that question.

Checking in: In this situation, there was an open invitation to independently reflect. We asked participants to think about a time they thought about their race at work. We let them know that in their breakouts they were only to discuss what they felt comfortable and safe sharing with their colleagues.

Asking broad, nonleading questions: After Jay noted that no one had ever asked about racist language at work, my cofacilitator and I asked the same question two times.

- To Jay: Is there something no one at the organization has asked you that you wish they would?
- To the whole group: Does anyone here have something they wish they'd been asked?

Validating without agreeing: To diffuse the awkwardness, my cofacilitator and I relied heavily on affirming statements, such as "What is landing with me right now is," "I am feeling transformed by hearing that," and "When you say that, I experience an emotion of . . ."

Sharing your perspective: In this case, sharing our perspective as facilitators meant synthesizing the many points raised by team members in the room, as well as playing back what we heard for clarifications, corrections, and responses.

Closing with care: We congratulated the team members for engaging in a difficult conversation collectively, thanked those who put their voices into the room, and encouraged next actions tied to asking questions about race regularly.

WITH CUSTOMERS OR CLIENTS

During the thick of the pandemic, I led a training on hidden bias and gender discrimination at a health-care company. Our training associate was involved in project managing every part of the session, including the follow-up message. In the email to attendees, she shared a recording of the session, additional resources, and a link to the survey. Her email signature contained a quotation from Ruth Bader Ginsburg with special importance to her: "Never underestimate a girl with a book."

The CEO of the client company responded by telling her the signature line flew in the face of everything we taught in the training session, that he was offended, and that no one would ever accept that quotation if the genders were swapped from "girl" to "boy." As the most junior member of my team interacting with a high-powered CEO figure, she was at a loss. She came to me asking what to do. I knew I would initiate a Compassionate Conversation with him, but before I did, I wanted to reach out to our immediate partner in the organization to let him know I would be taking this course of action. When I shared the email with him, he sighed deeply, and responded, "It's disappointing. I don't know what to tell you. He would never say that in person." As uncomfortable or charged as having live conversations about these issues may be, it's my opinion that absolutely nothing is harder than trying to find common ground over email. And yet, against the backdrop of the pandemic, a major sense of urgency on my part, and competing schedules, I used the Compassionate Conversations framework through email. Here's what it looked like.

Checking in: I started my email by noting the stressful season and challenges for health-care workers on his team during the pandemic. I asked if there was something I could do to support him during such a busy and intense time. I also let him know my teammate had sent his email across. Would he be open to having that discussion with me?

Asking broad, nonleading questions: Once he sent an affirmative response, I followed up with a few questions to ascertain where his resistance was coming from; was this an "I don't get it," "I don't like it," or "I don't like you" situation?

- What feelings did the Ruth Bader Ginsburg quotation invoke in you?
- What do you see as the relationship between the quote and the training?
- Are there elements of the training that did not resonate with you? Or are there elements of what we sent in the follow-up email that didn't add up?

Validating without agreeing: To give you a sense, the trusty Grammarly tone detector extension on my email labeled his response as "accusatory," "disapproving," and "forceful." In a nutshell, he felt discussions of hidden bias willfully ignored the bias he experienced as a man in the world. I affirmed that the training session did not contain examples of men facing bias and acknowledged how that might feel if he had gone through similar experiences in his own career. I thanked him for being so open. I checked *my* tone detector to make sure it sounded "friendly" and "confident." Then, I laid out my points.

Sharing your perspective: Starting with the phrase "Here's my perspective on the situation," I laid out what I considered to be the most important ideas I wanted him to consider.

I appreciate your question and your willingness to engage with the concept of inclusion. I wanted to call out a few thoughts relative to this quote in my teammate's signature line. Inclusion in the DEI framework refers to recognizing both equal opportunity and individual need. When we want to be inclusive, part of that is understanding who historically has not been included. In the case of this quote, women's literacy has actually not been equal to men's or a given until the second half of the last century. Recognizing and celebrating that is part of including women in the conversation around learning.

Perhaps even more importantly, though, I think this is an example to apply cultural awareness to. As you may have heard in her introduction, my teammate is a first-generation immigrant. I asked her why this quote was meaningful to her, and she shared: "I come from a country where female education is not always the focus and have seen positive change around that over the past decade. For me, this quote represents the [opportunities my parents gave me in my] childhood and the progress that my country has made in terms of female education."

Finally, I considered your point about if the gender identity was changed in the quote because I wanted to give it a proper thought. If the quote read, "Never underestimate the power of a boy with a book," I don't think it would be badly received because it's about childhood education. There's no specific underlying power dynamic that excludes boys from learning, and boys learning is not something that keeps girls from learning. Microaggressions are about reinforcing an existing power structure that keeps a group down, but celebrating the education of girls doesn't keep boys from learning or being educated.

Closing with care: I offered to meet over Zoom or initiate a phone call and said we'd incorporate more types of examples of bias in our next session together.

PART SIX

PERSONAL AND PROFESSIONAL FLOURISHING

MUCH OF THE MANAGEMENT WISDOM THAT exists today focuses on what you are supposed to be doing, whether it's listening more than speaking, volunteering for the toughest conversations, or demonstrating your expertise while remaining humble. But what about what *you* want to be doing? Understanding your own desires, motivations, and goals will help you avoid a trap many managers fall into: prioritizing their present-day job responsibilities over themselves. Throughout this book, we've delved into how to set healthy boundaries and consider your own emotions. Now, it's time to take all of those ideas and synthesize them into a tool kit for your personal and professional growth.

INVEST IN YOURSELF

Investing in yourself is a necessary part of demonstrating good leadership, continuously evolving your skills to better serve others, and being a valuable contributor to a team and organization. It's also a necessary part of ensuring you experience meaning, purpose, and belonging.

I have known many managers who quit their management jobs and switched into individual contributor roles. Several made the right choice—management wasn't the right path for a variety of reasons. Some, though, were adept, highly effective managers who lost the connection to their roles because of a lack of clarity, stress and burnout, or a disconnect between what they hoped for and what they saw happening around them. Leaving management wasn't their only choice, let alone the best choice. They just couldn't imagine something else.

Let me be clear: there is absolutely no shame in deciding to make a switch off a management track. We all go through different phases in our lives, and our preferences and priorities change. What this chapter aims to do is give you the confidence to know that being a manager and factoring yourself into the calculus around what the team needs isn't just an option; it's a strategy for a long-term career in the function.

> **INCLUSIVE MANAGEMENT TIP ELEVEN:**
> **WRITE YOUR IDEAL JOB DESCRIPTION**
>
> Use your management statement from part 1 to guide you through a more in-depth exploration of what you want management to look like for you. Set aside an hour to draft a job description for yourself that includes everything you might encounter in a normal posting: the type of organization you work for and its mission, an overview of your role, the roles and responsibilities associated with the role, the pay and benefits you receive,

and any work requirements. When it's complete, review it alongside your current job description. Where do they overlap? Where might you want to see a change in your current role to get you to your ideal one? How will you close that gap?

Access a template for your ideal job description at

alidamirandawolff.com/bookreaders.

27

WORK MIX AND DELEGATION

MANAGERS TEND TO SPEND MORE TIME in meetings than developing deliverables. New managers often understand this in theory and then in practice feel absolutely overwhelmed by the drastic change in their work mix. Going from a sprinkling of meetings a week mixed with time to work independently, all while sticking to a preplanned schedule, to the veritable chaos engine of too many meetings, too little time to follow up on them, and too few "as-planned" days creates backlogs and a sense of lowered self-efficacy. This phenomenon accounts for the steady stream of content on delegation that's perpetually circulated since people management became a function.

In your new role, develop a strong awareness of what your job actually entails day-to-day by assessing your work mix. Track how you spend your time each day and organize it by themes like "meetings," "budget and finance," "reporting and communications," and "special projects." Then, calculate what proportion of your days and week are spent doing that type of work, paying close attention to whether certain tasks took longer than you budgeted or expected. Use your analysis to compare how much work you have with the time allotted. A simple formula offers up a quick answer.

(Total Working Hours)
– (Average Hours in Allotted Breaks)
– (Average Hours in Weekly Meetings)
= (Total Independent Work Hours)

If you work an average of forty hours a week and take two regular thirty-minute breaks a day, plus you average about twenty-eight hours in meetings, then your formula will look like this:

40 Hours – 5 Hours – 28 Hours = 7 Hours

So, in your current work mix, you have seven hours left to follow up on meetings, put together presentations or project work, and address unexpected situations such as employee absences or resignations, accelerated deadlines, or urgent requests. Maybe this amount of hours works out because your role is well defined, your main job is to attend meetings, and your workflow is generally predictable. If that's true for you, go ahead and skip this section. If, however, you have ever felt you did not have enough time in a day to get everything done, keep going.

To solve for the problem of having too few available hours to do the work you need to, you have a few options:

1. Eliminate meetings and tasks.
2. Streamline meetings and tasks.
3. Delegate work to your employees.
4. Add resources to your team.

ELIMINATING

One of the greatest barriers to workplace equity is the sheer amount of work expected of employees. We confront this at Ethos constantly when analyzing the data; inclusion and belonging cannot take root in places where people are routinely overworked and underpaid. Even as productivity tools proliferate and new hacks for finishing work faster continuously evolve, employees find themselves in a state of continuous overwork and feeling overwhelmed. Broad-based structural and systemic changes to the way we perceive work and the power workplaces have over workers are the long-term solutions to this problem. In the short term, however, the first step to take for yourself is to review your meeting calendar and your job description . . . and cross things out.

Set a goal of eliminating 20 percent of your weekly meetings, and then eliminate another 20 percent of your weekly tasks. Bring these suggested edits to your own manager and paint a picture of what you will be able to accomplish with the newly freed up time. Chances are your manager won't approve all of the edits, but they may approve some and suggest others as well.

Let's also address the very real possibility that your manager isn't as focused on your holistic well-being and sense of belonging as you are. What do you do then? Start by cutting the things that are in your control and not in theirs. If you attend a biweekly status meeting with your teammates as a participant, go to every other meeting.

STREAMLINING

When elimination isn't possible, you may take an efficiency-based approach and streamline your weekly meetings and tasks. Set guidelines for meeting agendas, including how each meeting will be structured, how much time you have for it, and what format it should take. A standard agenda should include four components.

1. **Check in:** How are we entering the space? Are we settled and present? What do we need to say or do to feel settled and present?
2. **Meeting purpose:** What is the one thing we need to address in this meeting? If there is more than one item,

consider tabling it for another conversation or reserving it for later in the meeting if there is time.

3. **Core discussion:** What is the context around the one thing? What do we need to discuss, deliberate on, problem-solve, or decide? What is necessary to fully address the one thing?

4. **Check out:** What just transpired? What are our takeaways from the conversation? What do we need to do in the next few moments to go back into the world?

Still, even more meeting streamlining can take the form of agreeing on a format for certain types of meetings, making sure there's a balance between those types.

CATEGORY	DESCRIPTION
ASYNCHRONOUS	This often takes place one-on-one or in small groups; occurs through an approved communication platform; does not require alignment or group decision-making.
FORUM	Ideas and views on a particular topic are discussed; everyone invited is encouraged to share.
PRESENTATION	In this "one to many" format, a person or small group presents information for the participants to process. Participants do not have to share and may be expected to follow up after they have time to consider the information.
SYNC	Small groups meet to discuss and align on specific tasks, priorities, systems, or materials. These are often, but not always, delegation or decision-making meetings.
TRAINING	One or two facilitators lead a session of fifty minutes or more on a topic explained through one-third content, one-third small group exercises, and one-third large group discussion.
WORKING SESSION	Working sessions must contain three elements: work on deliverables or materials is performed in the meeting, alignment on those deliverables takes place, and clear next steps and owners are decided by the end of the meeting.

You can apply streamlining practices to your independent tasks as well. You might utilize automations to set up ongoing communications, update your project management platform, or generate timelines for yourself. You might also audit all of your tasks and look for ones that could be stacked or bundled together so that shared components are done only once and at the same time, rather than separately. For example, if you have a task to write a program description for the website and another to write internal communications about the new program, you might just use the website description as the internal communication. This may seem obvious, but the reality is that when we have too much work, we lose touch with where there are redundancies among our tasks. The key is to look for where you might consolidate before you start doing the work. Adding priority flags to tasks can also help you triage when you have too much. Setting up "urgent," "high," "normal," and "low" priority flags and assigning them to tasks eliminates the decision fatigue of deciding what to do next.

DELEGATING

No management book would be complete without the big "D" of delegation. The whole premise of management is that by having one person in charge of assigning—delegating—work, the whole team can run more efficiently. Yet for most of the managers I work with, delegation is the hardest part of the job. Why?

"It'll be faster if I do it."

"That's the worst job. I don't want to make someone do that."

"They'll mess it up."

"It's not a good use of their time."

"If I give this work to someone else, I won't have any work to do."

"If I give this work to someone else, it'll look like I'm not doing anything."

"I'm a servant leader."

Any of these sound familiar? Instead of going through a point-by-point rebuttal of each reason given, I will remind you that you already decided you do not have the time to do the work you are delegating. So maybe it would be faster if you did it, but you can't. You can eliminate the work (if it's not a good use of your time or their time, it might not be a good use of *anyone's* time). If elimination is not an option, which we already established it wasn't, then you can offer feedback and coaching support along with the delegation (what would they need from you to *not* mess it up?) and reframe your attitude toward delegation altogether (a servant leader knows their employees cannot grow if they aren't trying new things and dealing with challenges themselves).

Now this argument for delegation does not exempt you from putting your inclusive management principles into practices. You must be very conscious of what you are delegating and to whom. People from marginalized groups are more likely to take on the usually ignored and unseen work necessary for a team's success. This phenomenon is so common that software engineering leader Tanya Reilly coined a term, **glue work**, to describe it. Glue work refers to all of the valuable work employees do to hold a team together and make it successful that isn't rewarded with promotions or recognition. Examples might include scheduling meetings, creating necessary documentation, streamlining processes, onboarding new team members, or liaising with other teams. Someone has to do this work, yet often no one has this listed in their job description. Reilly finds that, overwhelmingly, people from nondominant gender groups take on this work and are told they are not "technical enough" or "strategic enough" to advance, increasing management and pay gaps between genders.

You have the power and responsibility to delegate this type of work across team members instead of concentrating it among a few people. You should also factor these additional tasks into performance reviews and reward employees who do these tasks well. After all, if this is the work of holding the team together, to undervalue it sends a clear message: only look out for yourself.

ADDING RESOURCES

When work cannot be eliminated, streamlined, or delegated (usually because the team is overwhelmed too), then the only recourse is adding resources. Depending on the organization's competing priorities, budget constraints, or real versus stated value of whatever it is you are trying to accomplish, adding resources may become a complex negotiation. What's important for any negotiation is to come prepared with a well-reasoned case for why you need what you're asking for, as well as several options should your top choice not be feasible.

Let's say you determine that the only way to meet a key project deadline and maintain the project over time is to add a full-time person to the team. The addition of a new hire is not in your department budget. Start your request with the ideal situation; don't negotiate against yourself ahead of time and come in with a compromise before the discussion begins. Instead, make sure that you can demonstrate exactly what you would need and why. Then, come prepared with your second, third, and fourth choices. If you cannot get approval for a full-time, dedicated employee, what about temporarily moving an employee from a different team onto yours for the project duration? Bringing on a part-time employee and extending the project timeline by six weeks? Hiring an outside consultant or agency to fulfill core needs? Paying overtime to everyone on your team who opts in to working longer hours until the project is complete? Investing in software and tooling that speeds up core tasks? You get the idea—there are always multiple options, and knowing what they are in advance increases the likelihood that you will get at least some of the help you need.

28

STRESS

KNOWING HOW TO ELIMINATE, STREAMLINE, DELEGATE, or add resources requires that you have at least some clarity. But in high-stress situations, you might find yourself going into autopilot mode, further perpetuating your stress and overwork. That's why understanding and managing your stress is so crucial.

Stress refers to any experience of emotional and physical tension. Often, a certain amount of stress motivates us to take action and pursue our goals and aspirations. This is a particular kind of stress, known as **eustress**, or good stress, when the gap between your current state and your desired future state requires you to push outside your boundaries. When you experience eustress, you feel uncomfortable, but you understand that the discomfort will lead to growth. It's usually characterized by feelings of hope, energy, and vigor. **Distress** is the opposite, the bad stress that results in extreme anxiety, discomfort, or pain. Distress is usually net negative, leading you to feel depleted and hopeless.

There are ten common forms of workplace stress contributors that you and your direct reports may encounter.

1. **Barriers to self-expression:** "I can't honestly say what I think or feel without repercussions."

2. **Lack of authority:** "I have many responsibilities but not enough authority to fulfill them."
3. **Limited time:** "I would perform at a higher level if I had more time."
4. **Lack of acknowledgment:** "I seldom receive acknowledgment or appreciation when I perform well."
5. **Dissatisfaction:** "I am not proud of my work or satisfied with my job."
6. **Discrimination:** "I have the impression that I am repeatedly discriminated against at work."
7. **Safety:** "My workplace environment is not safe."
8. **Work-life balance:** "My job often interferes with my family, social, and community commitments and personal needs."
9. **Conflict:** "I frequently argue with my teammates, leaders, or customers."
10. **Lack of control:** " I feel I have little control over my life at work."

While both eustress and distress can affect your sentiment toward work, another key factor is the actual *amount* of stress you feel. Eustress can become distress when the feelings of motivation transform into ones of anxiety. The Stress Curve[1] (see figure 4) demonstrates how easy this shift from one stage of stress, like optimum stress to overload, is as the stress level increases.

As the curve shows, when someone does not experience enough stress, they may be inactive or feel a sense of lethargy caused by "underload." An employee who recently finished a major project and awaits a new one might experience underload because they don't have deadlines to worry about, but they also don't have anything motivating them. Inactivity or underload are fine for short periods of time; they can even open time for rest, restoration, and leisure.

Optimum stress happens when someone experiences a moderate amount of eustress, which leads to high performance. When at

The Stress Curve

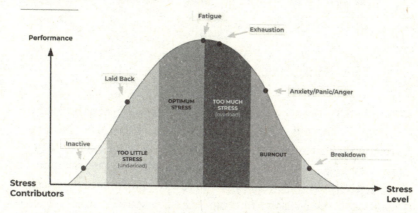

FIGURE 4

the optimum stress stage, an employee may feel fatigued at the end of the day but with a good night's sleep and some decompression time come back feeling refreshed and motivated.

The shift from fatigue to exhaustion often marks the beginning of overload, where the amount of stress affects performance quality and well-being. Instead of feeling fatigued and then ready to return after some rest, an exhausted employee may wake up tired and anxious about their workday. In some cases, that employee may feel exhausted only in the context of work, demonstrating that it's the psychological experience of doing the work causing the physiological impact, rather than something purely physiological. The move from overload to burnout and breakdown is a rapid and steeply downward-sloping curve. By the time burnout occurs, moving back up the curve to optimum stress becomes almost impossible.

You might struggle to notice when you are approaching the overload or burnout stages. First-time managers are susceptible to overload and burnout because they have so many types of stressors to contend with at one time. A new manager balances the responsibilities of their job with the on-the-job and off-the-job learning they have to do to fulfill those responsibilities, along with the emotional stress of navigating change.

TREATING STRESS
AND AVOIDING BURNING OUT

So what do you do if you start to experience overload or find yourself in the burnout zone? Our cultural conversation about burnout focuses almost solely on exhaustion, yet the experience of being overextended is simply not the same as being burned out. Specifically, when psychologist and researcher Christina Maslach developed the Maslach Burnout Inventory, she identified three components to burnout:

1. **Exhaustion:** A feeling of being constantly drained of energy at work due to being overextended. The experience of exhaustion dissipates when the worker leaves their workplace, either temporarily or permanently.
2. **Depersonalization:** A feeling that those you are meant to serve—customers, clients, students, volunteers, and so on—are problems rather than those you are meant to help. The term "depersonalization" is used interchangeably with "cynicism."
3. **Lack of personal accomplishment:** A feeling that your work accomplishes or contributes nothing, which can be associated with so-called "bs" jobs.

So why the hyperfocus on exhaustion? In part, it's because it's the easiest part of burnout to treat. You can take a vacation, get some sleep, advocate for fewer hours, hire more people, and share administrative tasks. These are all common recommendations for solving the problem of burnout, and while they have their merits, they may be totally ineffective when considered with what burnout really is. As a first-time manager, you might feel tempted to respond to your own burnout (not to mention your employees') with paid time off. That simply may not be the solution. Exhausted workers tend to have negative perceptions of their workload but not of the people they work with. Cynical workers, however, tend to have negative perceptions of their coworkers and work environments. Working less may not actually help a burned-out worker because their feelings of cynicism have totally alienated them from why they do the work in the first place.

It's worth noting that everyone from the original coiner of the term "burnout," psychologist Herbert Freudenberger, to Christina Maslach to author and burnout researcher Jonathan Malesic have identified that those who burn out tend to be idealistic because no matter how hard one works, those ideals fail to be met. Anecdotally, I see higher rates of burnout among people who ensure the well-being and care of others. In my research interviews with these individuals, they describe directly or indirectly that the ideal of "care" is one that can never be met. Disconcertingly, this might mean that our focus on "purpose-driven" work might be one of the biggest contributors to our culture of burnout, both in creating the conditions for more people to experience burnout and the idea that burnout is inherently a sign of worthiness.

If burnout is this gnarly, complicated problem you have to solve for yourself, what is the solution? Happily, the answer lies in part 2 ("Creating a Culture of Belonging"), with a twist. Because of its emphasis on personal value, group acceptance, and mutual support, belonging can serve as an important balm to burnout. In many ways, belonging and burnout are incompatible. Belonging requires a healthy sense of connection and mutuality. What matters in this case is how you seek out your own sense of belonging. You can apply the same Three Rs framework to yourself.

Relationships refer to your experience of positive, meaningful ties to your own colleagues, customers, and community members. The cultivation and maintenance of these relationships is a balm to feelings of cynicism because we remain committed to and connected to others. In practice, strong working relationships might translate into yes answers to these questions:

- If I experience an emergency, will others believe me and offer support? Will I have someone to turn to?
- When I feel stuck or confused, am I met with understanding and resources?
- Do others acknowledge and validate me as the person I am, in addition to the things I do?
- Do I feel I can offer help, encouragement, and acknowledgment to others? Will they receive this help, encouragement, and acknowledgment openly from me?

Resources are what you require to have the time needed to invest in relationships, though new managers tend to be chronically underresourced due to a lack of institutional knowledge and an often pervasive attitude of the need to "pay your dues." Nevertheless, when we are well resourced, we are less likely to be overextended or exhausted. Resources include the time and energy needed to regularly check in, offer and receive help, and praise and be praised. They also include money, tools, and services. How can I feel valued and respected if I know I am paid less than a colleague doing the exact same role? If my team is understaffed and I am pulling double shifts regularly, will I have enough energy to participate in the work community to feel part of something greater than myself?

To achieve a sense of belonging and stave off the exhaustion of burnout, it's worth making a list of everything you need to go from being overwhelmed to neutral. Some questions to ask are:

- Do I have clearly defined roles and responsibilities? Do I know what the "must-have" and "nice-to-have" components of my role are?
- Do we have enough staff support to complete our current list of projects?

- If I am unable to complete all of my work within a reasonable amount of time, do I have options other than working late, such as reaching out to a colleague, pushing a deadline, or hiring outside help?
- Am I authorized to automate manual tasks?
- Do I believe I am paid fairly relative to my colleagues?

Reciprocity is sometimes the hardest for managers because of the need to acknowledge power dynamics. The difference between reciprocal versus transactional workplaces is nuanced and important. Transactional relationships are transparent but not necessarily trusting. "If I stay thirty minutes late to help you with a problem, you will have to stay thirty minutes late next week when I ask. If you break that contract, our 'trade' relationship is over."

Reciprocal relationships are often transparent and always trusting; they are rooted in the belief that while not everything about our future interactions is known, I am confident that you will uphold my dignity and I yours. So maybe I need you to stay late today to help me with my problem, but when you need the same help next week, I can't stay because of a family commitment. In this case, I may enlist a fellow colleague to help you, brainstorm ideas ahead of time, bring you a prepared dinner to take home to alleviate stress, or take a pass on this situation but come through on another one.

Reciprocity is hard because it's both situational and long term; the only way to really establish true reciprocity is through the everyday muscle memory of making promises and keeping them, knowing one another, and being known. In this way, it can serve as a bulwark against lack of personal accomplishment because the strength and stability of your workplace relationships is an accomplishment.

29

ADVANCEMENT AND ALLYSHIP

MY FAVORITE BOOK ON IDENTITY AND solidarity is *Elite Capture* by the philosopher Olúfẹ́mi O. Táíwò. Despite its seemingly nefarious title, the book's core message can best be summed up with a single quotation:

"We also have to decide collectively where we're going, and then we have to do what it takes to get there. Though we start from different levels of privilege or advantage, *this journey is not a matter of figuring out who should bow to whom, but simply one of figuring out how best to join forces*" (my emphasis).

While Táíwò's words directly speak to the opportunity and possibility inherent in building a coalition of diverse people more focused on a shared goal than on how to hold power, they also underscore an important message about inclusive leadership. Advancement and allyship are not separate tracks. Your promotion does not have to come at the expense of your employees'; their success does not exist outside of your own. Throughout this book, I have taken care to emphasize the importance of balancing individual interests and group needs precisely because the modern, inclusive, equitable manager should not follow old rules about commanding, overseeing, and policing employees.

Understand that your next promotion, pay raise, or career move will come from how well you guide your team. High-output management as a concept came about to describe managers who know how to get the most from their teams. But your employees don't want you extracting their time, talent, energy, and labor, and if you're reading this book, then you don't want to do that to them. So here's a proposed revision. Humane high-output management means allying with the people who manage so that you may all achieve the best outcomes possible individually and for your organization. You can "win" by treating your employees with dignity and respect, accompanying them and supporting them through difficult moments, and celebrating with them in happy ones. Cultivating a culture of belonging for a diversity of people who hold different identities, beliefs, and values allows you to care for yourself, your employees, and the world, all at once.

INCLUSIVE MANAGEMENT TIP TWELVE: OPEN DOORS

If you are reading this book, it's because you've achieved some professional success. Take a moment to think about how you've done it. Then consider who in your organization or broader community you don't spend as much time with or don't counsel. Do they hold different identities than you? Would they benefit from knowing how you achieved your success? Go out of your way to connect with these people. Humbly share what you know.

CONCLUSION

AS MUCH AS THIS BOOK PRESENTS EXAMPLES and scenarios in the hopes of preparing you for the unexpected personal and professional challenges that leading a team of people brings, the truth is that regardless of what kind of manager you are or what specialization or expertise you hold, your day-to-day now revolves around the needs, conflicts, challenges, successes, questions, and frustrations of others. You will not be able to anticipate all of the situations you will encounter. Sometimes, you will make mistakes. Sometimes, you will hurt people's feelings, say the wrong thing, or even cause harm. Sometimes, others will hurt or harm you. And sometimes, you will profoundly change and be profoundly changed by those you manage.

All of these things are true because management is fundamentally about relationships. There is nothing more influential or transformational than how we interact with the people around us. There is also nothing more complicated. Our communities shape all of us, and your workplace has now become the community you steward. Cultivating and nurturing healthy, meaningful relationships offers so many possibilities. For the managers who take time and care to tend to their workplace communities, the effects of these changes extend far beyond the confines of one job or organization.

Throughout *The First-Time Manager: Diversity, Equity & Inclusion*, I've invited you to reflect on your own experiences with past managers, along with your hopes and aspirations for yourself. In that process, you may have remembered the small and big ways others poured into you and formed a clear picture of how you want to be the same. Keep those memories and ideas close. Think about how you can honor all that you received in order to get to the place you are in now and all you can give to others in turn.

But most of all, if you take anything away from this book, let it be this: becoming an inclusive manager means becoming a better person. In the process of your own "becoming"—becoming a first-time manager, a self-assured leader, a better person—you have an opportunity to shape who others become too. This is an enormous responsibility. What you do and say, how you are in your ways of working and being, all offer your employees a model of what they might be. Even those employees who you find it hard to connect with or understand will take something from you. Let it be something you would be proud to pass on.

ACKNOWLEDGMENTS

I learned an important lesson when I wrote and published my first book: an acknowledgments section is more about a moment in time and the people who were there with you than it is about the many, many, many people who deserve gratitude, consideration, and praise over the course of a lifetime. If I tried to honor the latter, this section would be twice as long as the manuscript itself.

With that, here is my humble attempt at thanking the people who most immediately affected my writing process. I wrote this book between March and June of 2023, and during that time, my team members at Ethos created space, offered support, and in many cases, directly contributed to and advanced the ideas featured here. To Angela Calise, Britney Robertson, Ivana Savic-Grubisich, Karen Thomas, Karyn Oates, María Emilia Lasso de la Vega, Miriame Cherbib, Sonni Conway, and Taryn Mortimer, thank you for being the team I've most trusted and appreciated in my professional career. Your ideas and practices inspire me each day, and many of them have been featured in this book.

I owe special thanks to some of these team members for the content contributions they made to this book. Karen Thomas and Miriame Cherbib originated innovations and refinements to the Compassionate Conversations framework, which made it so much better than what I had originally conceived. Additionally, watching them teach our "Understanding Your Role as Managers" course helped me simplify and enhance discussions of the power managers hold. Karyn Oates and her thorough and continuous work on inclusive language shaped that entire section of the same name; several of the examples I use in the inclusive language alternatives tables are directly hers or inspired by her work. I credit María Emilia Lasso de la Vega for helping me visualize difficult concepts in easy-to-read and accessible graphics, as well as making technical sections on accessibility and disability justice practical and actionable for new managers. This book would not have made it to market without Sonni Conway, who made the project to manage the book, the business, and me during this period into an art form. Sonni also went above and beyond in helping design the cover to meet accessibility and color contrast guidelines.

Other people critical in getting this book to press include my agent, Marilyn Allen, my editor, Tim Burgard, and my publicist, Dana Kaye.

To my guinea pigs for this entire inclusive management methodology—1871, WMNTech Cohorts 1–10, dscout, and the Poetry Foundation—your willingness to learn about inclusive management is the reason I have this book at all.

To my reader, Taylor Morrison, I aspire to be as multifaceted, self-aware, and humane as you in my leadership.

Esmé Weijin Wang was my writing teacher and coach on other creative nonfiction projects during this time. The methods and tools she offered for capturing and indexing information for an essay on grief and loss are a major part of how I made my deadline on this book.

My best friend, Katina, is my eternal idea tester; without her, I'd have a bunch of one-sided arguments and not nearly enough rigor behind my assertions.

I owe love and gratitude to my mom, who has approached my self-doubt about writing another book with the simple encouragement, "You will do it; you're the best." Thank you for always genuinely believing I'm the best, especially when I don't believe in myself.

My husband, Isaac, is a serial enabler who never casts judgment when I bring home a new massive project with no plan to eliminate other commitments. It's a testament to our partnership that he understands how much I need to create new things, and how willing he is to take up other responsibilities to make this possible.

I wrote a version of this book with my infant son, Tristan, wriggling on top of me during my parental leave. T, I love you more than anything, and I know you probably won't be interested in this book, if at all, for another twenty years. Still, it's for you.

GLOSSARY

Active listening is a technique developed in 1957 by Carl Rogers and Richard Farson to facilitate better collaboration in workplaces through a combination of practices, including listening for total meaning by observing verbal and nonverbal cues, recognizing shifts in the speaker's telling, understanding the speaker's perspective, and upholding the integrity of one's own perspective and interpretation.

Affiliative leaders are leaders who express care and interest in their teammates. They dedicate time and energy to creating a harmonious, warm, and welcoming environment.

Age is a social identity category that refers to how old you are and the generational cohort to which you belong.

Belonging is the experience of feeling as though you are part of something greater than yourself that values and respects you and that you value and respect back.

Belonging Action Plan is a tool for setting up regular team behaviors to foster belonging that documents the opportunity for change, the proposed practice to put in place, and a clear timeline for the practice's implementation.

Body type and size is a social identity category that refers to the physical characteristics of your body, including weight, height, and shape.

Boundaries are the emotional property lines that separate your thoughts and feelings from those of other people.

Caregiver status is a social identity category that includes people who take care of dependents without receiving compensation.

Coaching leaders take a personalized approach to upskilling their team members, resulting in long-term strategic capabilities.

Cultural awareness involves understanding the differences between us and people from other cultures or other backgrounds, especially differences in attitudes and values. Cultural awareness also involves becoming aware of our cultural values, beliefs, and perceptions to create space for those of others, usually by being willing to shift our own cultural context instead of asking others to assimilate.

Directive leaders tell employees what to do and how to do it, which results in alignment and clarity.

Disability is a social identity category that includes people who experience functional limitations in activities such as walking, talking, seeing, hearing, or learning.

Discrimination is defined as the unequal treatment of members of various groups based on conscious or unconscious prejudice, which favors one group over others based on differences of race, gender, economic class, sexual orientation, physical ability, religion, language, age, national identity, and other categories.

Distress, or the "bad stress," is the type of stress that results in extreme anxiety, discomfort, or pain.

Diversity simply means variety, and it's specific to the composition of a group. At work, diversity means the presence of difference within our contained environments.

Education level is a social identity category that refers to the level of education an individual has completed.

Employee Assistance Programs are benefits provided by some organizations that offer employees access to a third-party set of free and confidential resources like short-term counseling, referrals, advisory services, and other follow-up services for employees.

Employee power is the idea that employees can exert their power in an organization by withholding their labor, working less, or stopping work completely in order to create leverage with their employers.

Equal pay means paying the same salary to people performing the same role.

Equity encompasses equal access and the meeting of individual needs. Equity is a set of processes that seeks to ensure that everyone on a team not only has the same opportunities as others but that they can take advantage of them.

Ethnicity is a social identity category that refers to a group sharing cultural traits, such as the same language or customs.

Eugenics is a discredited, unscientific, and racially biased method to arrange reproduction within a human population to increase the occurrence of subjectively determined "desirable" characteristics. Eugenics was used as a justification by the Nazis for their treatment of Jewish, disabled, gay, and Roma people, as well as other nondominant groups.

Eustress, or "good stress," is a kind of stress characterized by feelings of hope, energy, and vigor.

A fishbowl conversation is a specific meeting format where a number of chairs are arranged in an inner circle, called a fishbowl, and the remaining chairs are arranged in a circle outside of the fishbowl. The main dialogue takes place between those in the fishbowl, with those in the ring around them observing and asking questions.

Foundational belonging refers to the inherent belief that everyone has a shared humanity that should be honored.

Gender is a social construct and social identity. It relates to attitudes, feelings, and behaviors a culture subjectively associates with an individual's biological sex.

Gender identity describes an individual's psychological sense of their own gender and may or may not correspond with the individual's sex assigned at birth.

Glue work is a term coined by software engineering leader Tanya Reilly to describe all of the valuable work employees do to hold a team together and make it successful that isn't rewarded with promotions or recognition.

Group belonging is the kind of belonging that managers are most expected to cultivate on their teams.

Hidden discrimination is behavior that may not be intentionally discriminatory or not perceived as such by the individuals doing the discriminating, while it may be perceived as offensive by the person being discriminated against.

Implicit bias is the negative association expressed automatically that people unknowingly hold and that affects understanding, actions, and decisions.

Inclusion allows individuals with different identities to feel they are invited into the group because they are valued, relied upon, and welcomed.

Intersectionality is a framework that allows us to understand how a person, group of people, or social problems are affected by a number of intersecting discriminations and disadvantages.

Involuntary termination occurs when an organization parts ways with an employee, whether by firing them or including them in a layoff. Employees do not elect to leave an organization in the case of involuntary termination.

The Model Minority Myth refers to a sociological phenomenon that generates a hierarchy among racial groups, pitting them against one another by positioning so-called "model" groups as economically and socially stable, if not upwardly mobile, in order to reinforce the existing racial supremacy of the dominant group.

National origin is a social identity category that refers to a person's immigration and citizenship status.

Nonviolent communication is also called the "language of compassion" and refers to the technique originated by Marshall Rosenberg that focuses on presenting communication in terms of observations, feelings, needs, and requests.

Pacesetting leaders set and meet their own high standards, exemplifying the quality, pace, and output they hope to see from their employees.

Participative leaders focus on generating consensus among employees through shared goal setting, visioning, and decision-making.

Pay transparency is publicly publishing what pay is. The process may involve publishing only salary ranges on job descriptions, publishing pay bands inside of the organization, or publicly listing all compensation.

Performance Improvement Plan is the proper term for documentation that a manager creates with specific details about an employee's underperformance, required actions the employee must take to improve, and a consequence—usually a termination date—should they fail to take those required actions.

Phrenology is a debunked pseudoscience involving the detailed study of the shape and size of the cranium as a supposed indication of character and mental abilities.

The Platinum Rule is to treat others how *they* want to be treated.

Political affiliation, sometimes referred to as party affiliation, refers to whether you belong to a certain political party.

Power is being able to do what you want to do or have others do what you want them to do.

Protective hesitation refers to the phenomenon whereby leaders avoid giving feedback for fear of seeming prejudiced against one or more social identity groups.

Race is a social identity category that refers to a group of people who are viewed as sharing the same physical traits.

Reasonable accommodation is a term that refers to the legal obligation organizations have to make adjustments that allow an employee to perform the essential functions of the job, as long as it does not create undue hardship for the organization.

Religion refers to the system of faith or worship you practice and may include not practicing any system.

SBIQ (Situation, Behavior, Impact, Question) is a feedback framework where the person giving feedback provides the context of the situation, names behaviors the person receiving feedback exhibited, explains the impact of those behaviors and why they warrant feedback, and asks a question to open up dialogue.

Self-belonging is the feeling of connection to ourselves.

Sex, which is often broken into the binary of "male" or "female," refers to the assignment a doctor gave a baby upon birth.

Sexual harassment, according to the Equal Employment Opportunity Commission, refers to unwelcome or unwanted sexual advances or conduct that impedes a person's job performance or creates a hostile, intimidating, or offensive work environment.

Sexual orientation relates to an individual's sexual and emotional attraction, behavior, and/or resulting social affiliation with others.

Social identity is a kind of identity you hold because you belong physically, mentally, and emotionally to a broader social group. Your social identity is directly tied to whether others see you as part of that social group.

Societal belonging occurs when people feel that society's structures and codes affirm them.

Socioeconomic status is a social identity category that relates to a person's class and household income.

The Three Rs are relationships, resources, and reciprocity.

> **Relationships** are meaningful connections between two or more people that result in feelings of acceptance, trust, and care.

> **Resources** refer to all the things employees need to be able to form meaningful relationships.

> **Reciprocity** means that within the ecosystem of your team, everyone is engaged in mutual give-and-take.

Tribal or indigenous status is a social identity category that refers to whether you are affiliated with, enrolled in, and belonging to a Native tribe or indigenous group.

Unconscious bias is when people, outside of their immediate conscious awareness, associate stereotypes with certain groups.

Visionary leaders define the ideal future, but they do not prescribe how to get there.

Voluntary termination occurs when an employee resigns from an organization or leaves of their own volition.

INCLUSIVE MANAGEMENT TIPS

Templates for practicing Inclusive Management Tips are available at alidamirandawolff.com/bookreaders.

INCLUSIVE MANAGEMENT TIP ONE:
LEARN FROM SUCCESS

We often learn from success better than we do failure, though we are cognitively wired to remember failure more distinctly. As you consider how you will become an inclusive manager, observe other managers as they manage their teams. Keep an active log of their most effective, constructive behaviors and consider how you might implement them yourself. You can access a sample log that includes examples of what to look for at:

alidamirandawolff.com/bookreaders.

INCLUSIVE MANAGEMENT TIP TWO:
CRAFT A MANAGEMENT STATEMENT

Imagine your highest vision of yourself as a manager. Write down a few sentences about what being a caring, inclusive, and just manager means to you, including what practices you might employ on a daily, weekly, monthly, and annual basis. Take some time to edit whatever you came up with into an easy-to-remember statement, preferably no more than six sentences. Then, print it out and frame it, use it as a desktop background, make it your phone home screen, or do all three! Whenever you are faced with management decisions, challenges, or even questions, go back to this statement and use it to help guide your next actions.

INCLUSIVE MANAGEMENT TIP THREE:
PRACTICE SELF-REFLECTION

One simple exercise that can help you create a culture of belonging is to reflect on a time you were part of a team—whether professionally, through volunteering, or other group activities—and list the specific behaviors that helped you feel like you belonged there. How did you know you belonged? What feelings did you experience? Similarly, reflect on a time when you felt you *didn't* belong. What was communicated in that situation, implicitly or explicitly, that triggered this feeling? With this data in mind, consider how you might adopt or eliminate practices on your own team to maximize a sense of belonging. Before you introduce them, invite your teammates to do the same exercise. Together, determine what practices to adopt or attempt.

INCLUSIVE MANAGEMENT TIP FOUR:
BECOME THE TEST CASE

There's nothing like firsthand experience to help illuminate the benefits and drawbacks of a particular experience. As you design work environments for your team members, start by testing out your ideas on yourself. For example, if you want to try out a new interactive polling tool for the next all-team meeting, start by using it in a smaller test environment. Ask yourself: "Does this add to the experience, like adding in a gaming component to the conversation? Or does it create unforeseen consequences, such as redirecting me out of my videoconferencing app and away from people's faces?" While this may seem like basic advice, remember that the temptation to just do things without trying them out first will be strong as you manage competing priorities. But managers who take the time to develop their ideas before implementing them are much more likely to have credibility with their team members and facilitate better experiences.

INCLUSIVE MANAGEMENT TIP FIVE:
START BY ASKING

When in doubt, start by asking your employees how they identify and why. Make sure to give them a clear "opt-out" if they don't want to engage in the discussion, and help prepare them for the experience by naming your own identities, at least the ones that matter to you most. Why the need to opt out? Depending on the circumstances, place, and time, it may not be safe or desirable to name these identities. The last thing you want is to force an employee to "out" themselves as an identity they are choosing to cover or conceal for safety reasons. As the legislative environment in the United States evolves to severely restrict the rights of trans people, for example, pronoun usage might actually put some of your employees at risk.

INCLUSIVE MANAGEMENT TIP SIX:
AVOID ASSUMPTIONS

Chances are that you have already gone through some form of unconscious bias training, which means you know that people associate stereotypes with certain groups that are outside of their immediate conscious awareness. Learning to "check your bias" is really developing the ability to pause before making an assumption about who someone is based on what identities they hold. After all, social identity is how others see you rather than how you see yourself. While you may have experience with people of a certain national origin, socioeconomic status, or education level, it is better to approach every employee with a mindset of curiosity.

INCLUSIVE MANAGEMENT TIP SEVEN:
PRACTICE ENGRAVING

Neuroscience shows us that when we closely watch others do something very well, we start to improve ourselves. For example, the singer Ray LaMontagne developed his distinctive artistic style by very closely and consistently listening to records of blues singers performing at their peak. If you want to develop a healthy feedback culture on your team, adopt this same approach by identifying a few people to watch—either ones you know and can observe in real time, or management experts online or at events. Practice adopting their phrases, mannerisms, and attitudes. Then, watch as your own employees do the same by watching you. You don't even have to tell them about engraving or observing how you give feedback; the nature of being a manager is that of receiving constant deliberate attention from the people working for you.

INCLUSIVE MANAGEMENT TIP EIGHT:
ENGAGE IN ROLE-PLAY

As you get used to giving team members feedback, one helpful practice is to role-play the scenario with a trusted peer. Fully commit to talking to that peer as if they are your employee, saying exactly what you plan to say. Take note of where you feel most uncomfortable, if there are different words or phrases you may want to use, and how your peer responds during and after the exchange. Avoid the draw of talking about the feedback you plan to give rather than acting it out; only with direct experience will you be able to tell if you are on the right track!

INCLUSIVE MANAGEMENT TIP NINE:
TRY AN AFTER ACTION REVIEW

To get your team into the habit of giving and receiving feedback across all levels and about different types of work, introduce an After Action Review, which is sometimes called a postmortem. This is a review where team members evaluate a project to develop insights that inform future projects by reflecting on its successes and areas for improvement. For major initiatives, adopting a regular After Action Review process strengthens a team's feedback culture while contributing to better project outcomes in the future. For an especially productive After Action Review meeting, complete a premeeting form to record individual feedback, host a moderated meeting with a designated facilitator, capture key, agreed-upon insights in easy-to-access space, and send a follow-up detailing how these insights are being used two to six weeks later. Access an After Action Review template at **alidamirandawolff .com/bookreaders**.

INCLUSIVE MANAGEMENT TIP TEN:
PRACTICE HEALTHY, STRUCTURED CONFLICT

Remove the stigma from conflict by creating spaces for healthy conflict, like fishbowl conversations. Present an idea, and ask team members to discuss and debate its merits. You might even consider assigning positions on the idea at random, asking those in support of an idea to argue against it and vice versa.

INCLUSIVE MANAGEMENT TIP ELEVEN:
WRITE YOUR IDEAL JOB DESCRIPTION

Use your management statement from part 1 to guide you through a more in-depth exploration of what you want management to look like for you. Set aside an hour to draft a job description for yourself that includes everything you might encounter in a normal posting: the type of organization you work for and its mission, an overview of your role, the roles and responsibilities associated with the role, the pay and benefits you receive, and any work requirements. When it's complete, review it alongside your current job description. Where do they overlap? Where might you want to see a change in your current role to get you to your ideal one? How will you close that gap? Access a template for your ideal job description at **alidamirandawolff.com/bookreaders**.

INCLUSIVE MANAGEMENT TIP TWELVE:
OPEN DOORS

If you are reading this book, it's because you've achieved some professional success. Take a moment to think about how you've done it. Then, consider who in your organization or broader community you don't spend as much time with or don't counsel. Do they hold different identities than you? Would they benefit from knowing how you achieved your success? Go out of your way to connect with these people. Humbly share what you know.

NOTES

CHAPTER 3

1. Loren B. Belker, Jim McCormick, and Gary S. Topchik, *The First-Time Manager* (New York: HarperCollins Leadership, 2021), 63.

CHAPTER 4

1. If you aren't sure what motivates your employees or how they respond to expectations, consider taking an assessment such as "The Four Tendencies" by author and researcher Gretchen Rubin. The assessment is available for free on her website: gretchenrubin .com/quiz.

CHAPTER 11

1. R. F. Baumeister and M. R. Leary, "The Need to Belong: Desire for Interpersonal Attachments as a Fundamental Human Motivation," *Psychological Bulletin*, 117, no. 3 (1995), 497–529, https://doi.org /10.1037/0033-2909.117.3.497.
2. If you are struggling to understand or practice foundational belonging, consider picking up a copy of Sharon Salzberg's *Real Love* to understand the basic tenets of loving-kindness.

CHAPTER 12

1. An abbreviated version of this section was published in the June print issue of *Talent Management*.

CHAPTER 13

1. Denise Brodey, "Only 4% of Employees Disclose a Disability, but New HR Tools and Training Could Upend That Trend," *Forbes*, November 8, 2022, https://www.forbes.com/sites/denisebrodey /2022/10/18/only-4-of-employees-disclose-a-disability-but-new -hr-tools-and-training-could-upend-that-trend/.

CHAPTER 14

1. Ideas adapted from an article I wrote for *Talent Management* called "Rethinking Progress: An Alternative Approach to Pursuing 'Bigger/ More' Goals" (https://www.talentmgt.com/articles/2023/02/08 /rethinking-progress-an-alternative-approach-to-pursuing-bigger -more-goals/).

CHAPTER 17

1. "Inclusive Language." n.d. 18F Content Guide. Accessed March 28, 2022, https://content-guide.18f.gov/our-style/inclusive-language/.
2. "Bans on Best Practice Medical Care for Transgender Youth," Movement Advancement Project | Health Care. Accessed June 18, 2023, https://www.lgbtmap.org/equality-maps/healthcare/youth _medical_care_bans.
3. Eitan Hersh, "How Many Republicans Marry Democrats?" FiveThirtyEight, June 28, 2016. https://fivethirtyeight.com/features /how-many-republicans-marry-democrats/.

CHAPTER 20

1. While the SBI framework was developed by the Center for Creative Leadership, the added "Q" is an innovation of Miriame Cherbib, an independent DEI practitioner and member of the Ethos team as of the writing of this book.

CHAPTER 26

1. This section has been adapted from my previous article for *Talent Management*, "Planning for the Worst: Compassionate Remote Layoffs" (https://www.talentmgt.com/articles/2023/04/26/planning-for-the-worst-compassionate-remote-layoffs/).

2. Les Leopold, "Op-Ed: Being Laid Off Is Devastating. Yet Society Never Measures That Toll," *Los Angeles Times*, January 17, 2023, https://www.latimes.com/opinion/story/2023-01-17/tech-layoffs-stress-trauma-unemployment-economy.

CHAPTER 28

1. "The Stress Curve," The Chelsea Psychology Clinic, April 23, 2018, https://www.thechelseapsychologyclinic.com/blog/see-stress-curve/.

INDEX

ABOUT THE AUTHOR

ALIDA MIRANDA-WOLFF is a diversity, equity, inclusion, and belonging (DEIB) practitioner committed to teaching love and cultivating belonging. She is the author of two books with HarperCollins Leadership, *Cultures of Belonging: Building Inclusive Organizations That Last* (February 2022) and *The First-Time Manager: Diversity, Equity, and Inclusion* (May 2024). She is the founder and CEO of Ethos, a full-service DEIB and  employee advocacy firm, which serves hundreds of clients across the world. Alida also hosts *Care Work with Alida Miranda-Wolff*, a podcast about what it means to offer care for a living.

In 2021, Alida received the University of Chicago's Early Career Achievement Award. She is a graduate of the University of Chicago and holds certificates from the School of the Art Institute (graphic design) and Georgetown University (DEI). She lives in Chicago with her partner, son, rabbits, and cats. When she's not working, reading, writing, or parenting, Alida is wild gardening, interior designing, and falling down research rabbit holes.